Appliqué Takes Wing

Appliqué Takes Wing

Exquisite Designs
for Birds, Butterflies,
and More

Jane Townswick

Martingale®
& COMPANY

Credits

President ◆ Nancy J. Martin
CEO ◆ Daniel J. Martin
VP and General Manager ◆ Tom Wierzbicki
Publisher ◆ Jane Hamada
Editorial Director ◆ Mary V. Green
Managing Editor ◆ Tina Cook
Technical Editor ◆ Cyndi Hershey
Copy Editor ◆ Ellen Balstad
Design Director ◆ Stan Green
Illustrator ◆ Laurel Strand
Cover and Text Designer ◆ Stan Green
Photographer ◆ Brent Kane

That Patchwork Place® is an imprint of
Martingale & Company®.

Appliqué Takes Wing: Exquisite Designs
for Birds, Butterflies, and More
© 2005 by Jane Townswick

Martingale & Company
20205 144th Avenue NE
Woodinville, WA 98072-8478 USA
www.martingale-pub.com

Printed in China
10 09 08 07 06 05   8 7 6 5 4 3 2

Library of Congress Cataloging-in-Publication Data

Townswick, Jane.
    Appliqué takes wing : exquisite designs for birds, butterflies, and more / Jane Townswick.
        p. cm.
     ISBN 1-56477-584-4
    1. Appliqué—Patterns. 2. Birds in art. 3. Butterflies in art. I. Title.
     TT779.T65 2005
     746.44'5041—dc22
                                        2004024062

Mission Statement
Dedicated to providing quality products
and service to inspire creativity.

Dedication

To Gail Kessler

For seeing something worthwhile in my appliqué during the days when I was carrying my blocks around in a pizza box, I am more grateful to you than I can express. Thank you for inviting me to teach classes at your wonderful quilt shop, Ladyfingers Sewing Studio, in Oley, Pennsylvania in 1997. Your encouragement, professionalism, and generosity of spirit have made it possible for me to enter a career in teaching, and your friendship means the world to me.

Acknowledgments

To Dot Murdoch and Teri Weed, my utmost gratitude for making all of the samples for the how-to photographs shown throughout this book. I am honored to have your incredible workmanship illustrate my designs and techniques.

Many thanks to my editor, Cyndi Hershey, for her talent and skill in making this a better book, and to everyone at Martingale & Company for its production.

Contents

Introduction

Are you ready to join me on an adventure in color-blend appliqué

and explore the beauty of birds and butterflies?

IF YOU ARE A BIRDER, you may already enjoy an ongoing panorama of inspiration in your own backyard, from robins to more colorful birds and butterflies, such as cardinals, blue jays, monarchs, cicadas, or luna moths. It's easy to blend an array of your favorite colors in similar values and interpret your favorite birds in hand appliqué.

In addition to color blending, I have developed a way to do transparent appliqué with specialty fabrics like metallic sheers, lamés, and meshes. The iridescent and see-through qualities of these fabrics make them perfect choices for stitching the delicate wings of a butterfly or moth. (Note that most quilt shops do not carry these types of specialty fabrics. You'll need to visit your local general fabric store, which should have a good supply, often in the bridal or fashion-fabric department.) The stumbling block that faced me initially was how to work with the fabrics without letting seam allowances show through. I came up with some interesting ways to make that possible, such as doing reverse appliqué on top of fabrics that have already been reversed appliquéd. I call this new technique double reverse appliqué. Check out the Dragonfly block on page 86, the Luna Moth block on page 97, and the Cicada Moth block on page 105, to see examples.

In this book, you will find twelve 9" block designs—six feature birds and six depicting butterflies or moths. With each block you'll find a list of the techniques you will learn as you stitch the design. The step-by-step photos will guide you visually as you select fabrics and put your own appliqué units together. "Gallery of Quilts" on pages 24-43 is filled with gorgeous quilts, wall hangings, and pillows that have been made by students who took classes with me at the Ladyfingers Sewing Studio in Oley, Pennsylvania. Spend some time browsing through these quilts and enjoy seeing the 12 designs interpreted in different colors and creative ways.

As you stitch your own blocks from the designs in this book, I hope you'll let your creativity run free and come up with innovative ways to combine them in settings that reflect your personal talents and abilities. Happy stitching!

Jane Townswick

Hand-Appliqué Basics

The more you love hand appliqué, the more you will enjoy discovering new tools and techniques. Check out the following list of the things I like for hand appliqué, and add the ones you find useful to your own list of favorites.

Tools and Supplies

Using the right equipment makes any quiltmaking task easier, more accurate, and more fun. Here are the tools and supplies I keep on hand at all times for hand appliqué.

- 9½", 12", and 15" square Omnigrid rulers
- 1" x 6", 3" x 18", and 6" x 24" Omnigrid rulers
- Large- and medium-sized rotary cutters
- 24" x 36" self-healing cutting mat
- Clover silk pins
- Jeana Kimball's Foxglove Cottage extra-sharp appliqué pins
- Jeana Kimball's Foxglove Cottage size 11 straw needles (see "Resources" on page 127)
- John James size 12 Sharp needles (see "Resources" on page 127)
- 100-denier silk thread by YLI, especially the neutral colors 212, 226, 235, and 238, and the coral color 217
- Natural beeswax
- Well-fitting thimble with a ridge around the top
- 4" bamboo skewers or round wooden toothpicks with sharp tips
- 3½" Gingher embroidery scissors with microserrated blade (for cutting fabric)
- Clover patchwork scissors (for cutting paper)
- Avery glue pen (for glue-basting fabric)
- Freezer paper, template plastic, and CAT paper* (for making templates)
- Sharpie permanent pen in black (for marking templates)
- Clover heat-removable white marking pen and eraser pen (for marking and erasing marks on fabric)
- Quilter's Choice silver pencil (for marking fabric)
- Pigma .01 mm marking pens in black and in colors (for inking fabric)
- Small wooden "finger-creasing" iron
- Clover Hera marker
- Multicircle stencil

* CAT paper (Clear Appliqué Template paper) is an opaque paper with an adhesive back that adheres easily to fabric. It is available from Ladyfingers Sewing Studio (see "Resources" on page 127).

Determining Thread Length

1. To make sure that you will be more comfortable while you stitch, start by determining the correct thread length for your own body. Hold the end of the thread between your thumb and index finger in one hand. With the other hand, pull the spool of thread gently down to your own elbow.

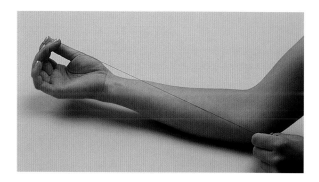

2. Cut the thread at that point and coat it with natural beeswax.

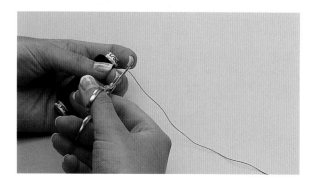

Anchoring Silk Thread onto a Needle

If you like the ease with which silk thread glides smoothly through fabric and allows you to make tiny stitches, follow these steps to anchor a strand of 100-denier silk thread onto the eye of a needle.

1. Start by threading a needle with thread cut to the correct length for you. Make a loop with the short end of the thread and insert the needle into the loop. With your right-hand index finger, hold the loop to the needle.

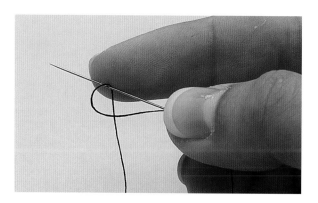

2. Take the tip of the needle in your left hand. With your right hand, gently pull on the long end of the thread, allowing the loop to slide down along the shank of the needle and "lock" onto the eye of the needle.

Anchoring Cotton Thread onto a Needle

If you prefer matching the fiber content of the thread to the cotton fabric you use for quilting, use this method to anchor cotton thread onto a needle.

1. To anchor cotton (or 50-denier silk) thread onto the eye of a needle, start by threading a needle with the thread cut to the correct length for you. Holding the needle in your right hand, pick up the short end of the thread between your left thumb and middle finger. Lay the thread over the fingernail of your left index finger, bringing it around your finger, and grasp the longer part of the thread together with the short end.

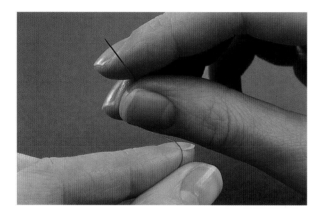

2. With the needle in your right hand, hold the threads in your left hand tightly so that the thread stays taut across your left index fingernail. Lay the needle flat on the surface of your fingernail at a 90°-angle to the thread. Point the tip of the needle at the thread. Slide the needle across the surface of your fingernail so that the tip of the needle just pierces the thread; then immediately stop pushing the needle.

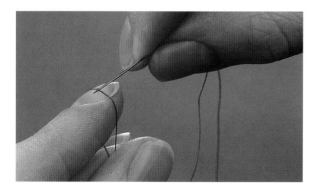

3. Hold the needle tip with your left hand and gently pull the long end of the thread down along the shank of the needle with your right hand. This will lock the thread securely onto the eye of the needle.

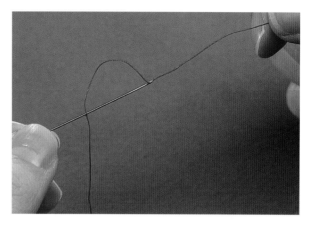

4. Whenever you end the thread, simply clip the thread just below the eye of the needle to release it.

Tying a Quilter's Knot

Whether you're about to appliqué, hand quilt, or even sew on a button, this is the simplest technique for creating a neat, small knot at the end of your thread.

1. Thread the needle. Hold the needle and the long end of the thread together in your right hand. With your left hand, gently wind the thread two or more times around the needle (six times for 100-denier silk).

2. Slide the wound threads down the shank of the needle so that they lie between your right thumb and forefinger. Then using your left hand, gently pull the needle all the way out from between your fingers so that the wound threads pull down to create a small, neat knot at the end of the thread.

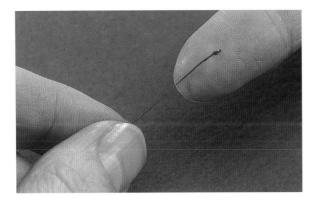

Starting to Stitch

With the needle and thread prepared, follow these steps to start appliquéing.

1. Cut a ³⁄₁₆" seam allowance around an appliqué shape and pin it in place on the background fabric. Bring the needle up just inside the marked turning line on the appliqué shape. Place your left thumb just under the thread at the marked turning line, and support the background and appliqué fabrics with your middle finger underneath.

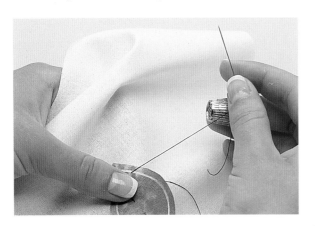

2. Using a bamboo skewer or round wooden toothpick with a sharp tip, gently tuck the seam allowance under, supporting it with your underneath middle finger. When you are happy with the way the folded edge of the appliqué shape looks, pinch the fabric gently between your thumb and underneath finger to make the fold crisp without distorting the fabric.

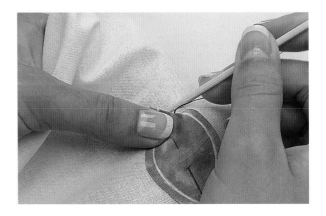

3. Pull the thread out at a 90° angle to the creased fold. Holding your needle vertically, insert it into the background fabric, just to the right of the thread and next to the folded edge of the appliqué shape.

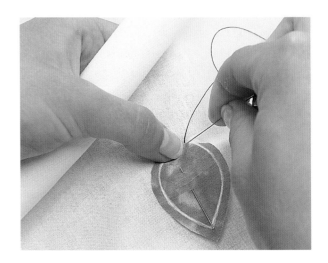

4. Gently lower your hand and arm from the elbow, without bending your wrist, so that the needle comes back up through the background fabric and catches the very tip of the fold on the appliqué shape. This easy, natural movement will allow you to establish your own perfect stitch length by working with the motions of your own hand and arm. It will also help you stitch more comfortably for longer periods of time and avoid causing repetitive stress on your wrist as you sew.

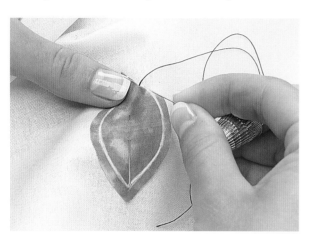

5. Pull the needle and thread out at a 90° angle to the fold of the appliqué shape again, as shown. This will show you the exact place to insert the needle for the next stitch: just to the right of the thread, and next to the fold. Continue making each appliqué stitch in the same manner.

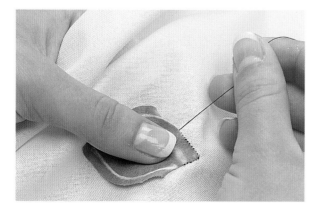

Ending a Thread

To end a thread, follow these steps.

1. Insert your needle into the background fabric as if you were going to take another stitch, but bring it all the way through to the wrong side of your work. Wind the thread around the needle two or three times, and insert the tip of the needle between the background fabric and the appliqué shape, as close as possible to your previous stitch.

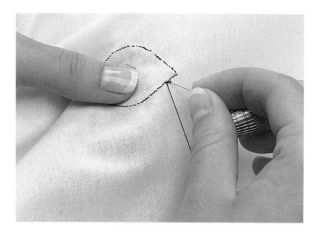

2. Pull the thread all the way out of the background fabric, leaving a small French knot on the surface.

3. Tug on the thread gently to pop the French knot between the background and appliqué fabric. Clip the thread close to the surface of the fabric.

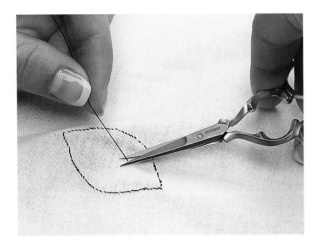

Finishing

All of the blocks in this book involve the same finishing techniques. After you finish stitching, take a moment to think about whether you want to do hand quilting inside of any of the larger appliqué shapes. If so, you can trim away some of the background fabric underneath those areas. To do this, take care to separate the layers of fabric carefully. Use a sharp pair of embroidery scissors to cut out the background fabric, allowing a ¼" seam allowance to remain inside each shape.

To give your appliqué a crisp finish, spray the back side of your work very lightly with water and press it with a hot, dry iron set at the cotton heat level. Spray the front side of your block with water and press it again. Be sure to use a cotton press cloth if your blocks contain a specialty type of fabric, such as metallic sheer, mesh, or lamé. Place the block on top of a rotary-cutting mat and center a 9½" square Omnigrid ruler over your work. Use a rotary cutter to trim the finished block to 9½" square.

Special Techniques

Whenever I want to come up with a new technique for hand appliqué, I like to start by considering the things that make a certain stitching task problematic and then develop ways to make it easier. The following techniques resulted from my struggles with traditional methods for stitching bias stems and vines, steep points, branches, and leaves. Try my methods on scrap fabrics and see if they please you.

Bias Stems and Vines

A perfect stem or vine starts with two accurate and parallel turning lines with a ⅛" seam allowance outside each line.

1. Place a square (size provided within a given pattern) of fabric on a cutting mat, with the *wrong* side facing up. Align the 45°-angle line on a 3" x 18" or 6" x 24" quilter's ruler with the lower edge of the fabric and rotary cut the fabric diagonally into two triangles. Lay a quilter's ruler over the diagonal cut edge of one triangle, aligning the ⅛" markings on the ruler with the cut edge of the fabric. Hold the ruler firmly in place with your left hand and place a Hera marker next to the ruler. Slowly and firmly, move the Hera marker back and forth across the fabric,

pressing down very hard to score a straight line ⅛" from the cut edge of the fabric. Because you're working on the wrong side of the fabric, the ⅛" seam allowance you're creating will automatically want to turn in the correct direction when you're ready to stitch the completed bias stem.

2. Move the ruler to the right of your first scored line, as far as your desired finished stem width. Align the ruler on top of the first scored line at this width and score a second line in the same manner as the first. This will give you two perfectly straight, parallel turning lines on the fabric.

3. Move the ruler ⅛" to the right of your second scored line and rotary cut the second seam allowance at that distance to complete the bias stem. Cut the short ends of the bias strip perpendicular to the long edges.

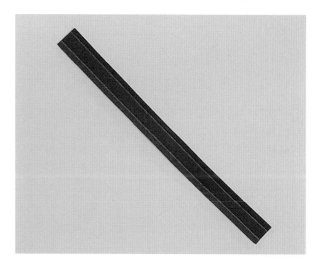

Free-Form Stems and Branches

I often like to stitch stems and branches with uneven edges for a more artistic look. Follow these steps to create your own free-form stems and branches.

1. For any of the free-form stems in blocks in this book, you can use the patterns given with each block, or be adventurous and simply cut your own free-form pieces. Start by cutting a ⅜" x 4" stem in any curvature you like.

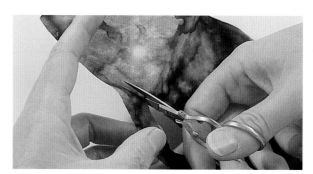

2. Appliqué one edge of this stem to a second piece of fabric in any color you like. I like to stitch inner curves first, but that is not a hard-and-fast rule. As you stitch, make clips into the stem at different depths so that the stitched edges will be random and not a straight line.

3. Cut the second fabric to approximately ¼" from the stitched line.

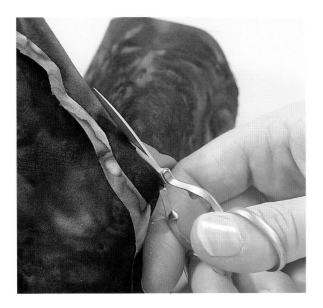

4. Lift up the first portion of the stem you stitched and trim the remainder of the second fabric next to the underlying seam allowance.

5. To add additional fabric layers for a wider stem or branch in a particular project, repeat steps 2–4.

*Y*OU CAN USE this free-form technique to create stems and branches of any width you like. Check out the branch in the Luna Moth block on page 97 and think about the possibilities of color blending a tree trunk with many different fabrics.

Steep Points

Several of the bird and butterfly designs in this book feature my steep-point technique. No matter what the appliqué shape, or how many fabrics are color blended in it, you can use this technique to stitch any steep point with ease.

1. Cut a ³⁄₁₆" seam allowance around a traced shape that has a steep point.

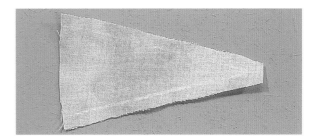

2. Stitch the *right edge* of the appliqué shape to the background fabric all the way up to the very tip of the point. Insert the needle into the background at the very tip and bring the thread all the way through to the wrong side of your work. Take a stitch on top of your last stitch and lock the thread securely by running the needle through the circle of thread as shown.

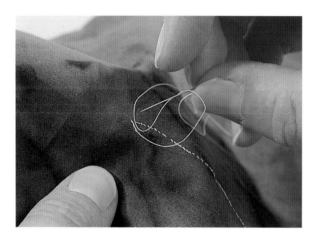

3. Clip the thread, leaving a 6" tail hanging on the wrong side of your work; you will need this thread to tie a knot after finishing the second side of the point.

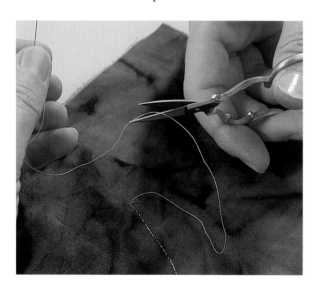

4. Clip the seam allowance on the unstitched edge of the appliqué shape, approximately ½" to ¾" down from the tip of the point. Turn under and stitch the seam allowance from the clip to the end of the appliqué shape.

5. On the wrong side of your work, you will need to cut the background fabric *only*. Starting approximately ¼" below the place where your stitching stops on the *unfinished* side of the appliqué shape, cut straight up to the very tip of the point. Also make a second cut over to (but not through) the stitched line, following the white lines.

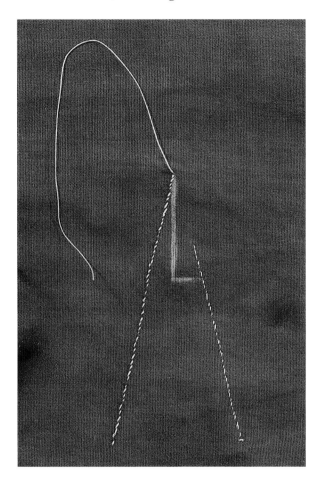

6. Using a bamboo skewer or toothpick, gently lift up the narrow L-shaped flap of background fabric and fold it over the partially stitched line.

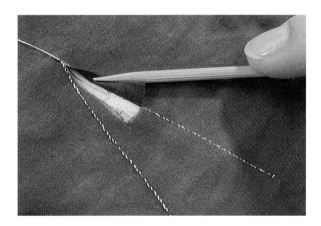

7. Press the fabric down very hard with your finger, creating a fold that will continue perfectly straight from your stitched line up to the point.

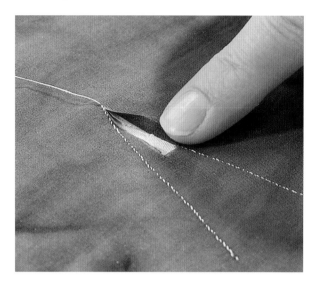

8. Continue finger-pressing until the entire L-shaped flap of fabric is creased all the way up to the tip of the point.

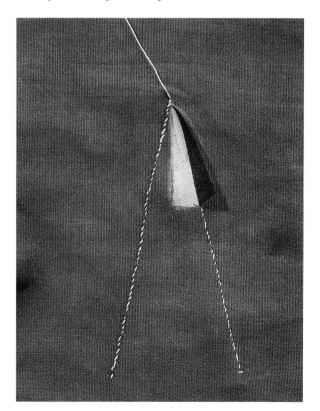

9. When you are happy with the way the folded edge looks, coat the tip of a bamboo skewer or toothpick with glue from a glue stick and run the glue underneath the fold. Then press the fabric in place with your finger to baste it in place.

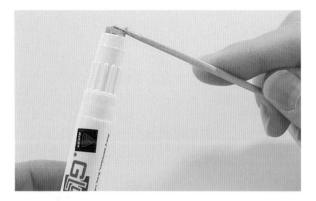

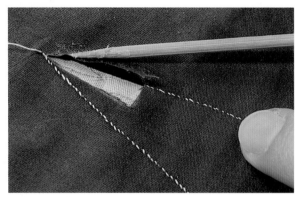

10. Pick up your work and use your left index or middle finger to push up the seam allowance of the point shape through to the wrong side of your work.

11. On the right side of your work, you will have a perfectly accurate, glue-basted fold at the unstitched area on the left side of the point shape. Thread a needle with thread that matches your background fabric and stitch this area to the appliqué shape, ending at the very tip of the steep point.

12. When you take the last stitch at the very tip of the steep point, take the needle all the way through to the wrong side of your work. Using this thread and the 6" tail of thread left hanging from step 3, tie two knots at the tip of the steep point and clip the threads close to the knot.

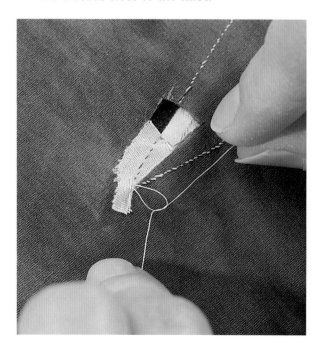

Color Blending Fabrics for Appliqué

You can express your own unique color preferences and give your appliqué richer visual depth by blending many fabrics of similar values within an appliqué shape. The key to this simple process is to use similar values (the lightness or darkness of a color) between neighboring shapes.

Here are some examples that illustrate my concept, along with guidelines to follow as you select fabrics for the designs in this book. After reading through them, gather some fabrics from your stash, and start playing with your own color and value sequences until you have an arrangement that pleases you.

1. Color value (lightness or darkness) is more important than color itself for color blending. Use similar values beside each other and they will blend together visually.

2. Sudden changes in color value draw the eye to a specific fabric in an appliqué shape. Unless you really wish to create this particular effect (which can be a creative option), avoid abrupt switches in value.

3. You can use small-scale multicolored prints, tone-on-tone fabrics, solids, hand-painted fabrics, batiks, or any other fabric that pleases you for color blending. As long as you keep color values similar between neighboring shapes, you can create exciting visual effects.

4. Avoid plaids or high-contrast prints for color blending. Fabrics like these tend to draw attention to themselves, which makes them less effective for color blending.

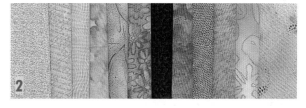

Gallery of Quilts

*The following pages will give you a glimpse into the glorious ways that
the blocks in this book can be combined to create beautiful appliqué quilts.
Each of the quiltmakers has taken one or more classes with me at Ladyfingers
Sewing Studio in Oley, Pennsylvania, where the first and foremost class rule is
to have fun stitching. Each month these talented quilters stitched a bird or
butterfly block by using new techniques such as transparent appliqué or double
reverse appliqué. They came up with color combinations that will wow you
and experimented with metallic sheer and mesh fabrics that resulted
in exquisite, gossamer wings. Take time to look at the quilts carefully,
and you will become acquainted firsthand with the vibrant personalities
of the quilt artists who made them.*

Jungle Jems
42" x 58"

Think outside the box while appliquéing these blocks. The challenge presented to us by Jane was to use fabric one seldom sees in quilts, such as chiffon, suede, or polyester. She taught the techniques necessary for dealing with these temperamental fabrics successfully. My husband, Bob, designed this setting. He used straight lines to create visual curves.

—*Kathy DeCarli of Downingtown, Pennsylvania*

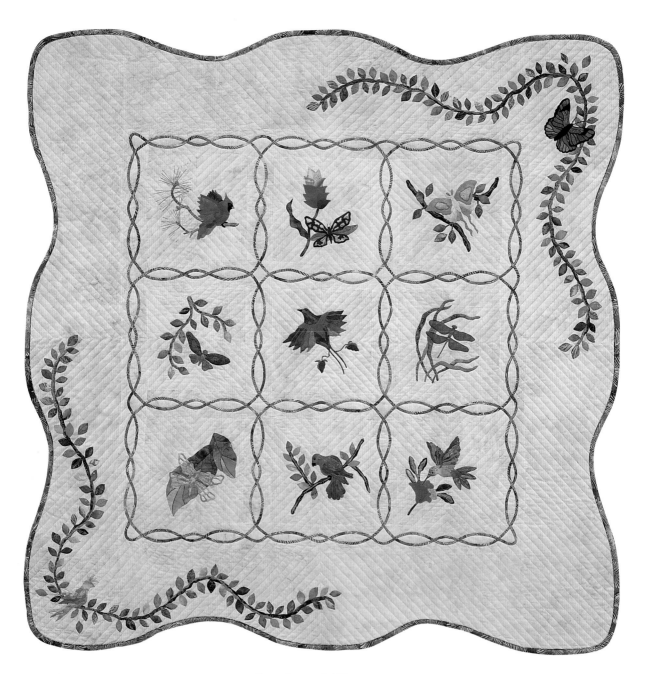

Broken Wings

69" x 69"

This quilt was a joy to make. It is called "Broken Wings" because two of the creatures have broken wings. Can you find them? I also was dealing with a broken wing of my own: as I began the quilting, I discovered I needed hand surgery, and what had once been a simple joy could no longer be taken for granted.

—Teri Weed of Wynnewood, Pennsylvania

Flights of Fancy
36" x 36"

I have always had the desire to paint. Jane's appliqué methods allow me to blend colors and achieve dimension, texture, and depth without a paintbrush. Now I can realize my dream with fabric instead of with paints and brushes. I thank Vera Kutz for her help with assembly, borders, and binding. This quilt was machine quilted by Janice Petre.

—Debi Kuring of Blandon, Pennsylvania

Midnight in the Forest
31" x 31"

I've always been cautious and used light, neutral fabrics for my backgrounds, but Jane put me over the top by encouraging me to try something different. It's really a great feeling to let your creativity break free. I thank Vera Kutz for her help with assembly, borders, and binding. This quilt was machine quilted by Janice Petre.

—Debi Kuring of Blandon, Pennsylvania

Wing It!
45" x 45"

I thank Dot Murdoch for getting me started and inviting me to join Jane's class. Oh, what fun I had for two years. Jane pushed us to explore and to do our own thing. Thank you, Jane, for letting us fly! And thanks to Carol Heisler of Lorac Designs for completing the quilt with her beautiful machine quilting.

—Jo Anne Yarnall of West Chester, Chester County, Pennsylvania

Sparkling Flying Objects
50" x 50"

This was my first appliqué piece. Since I knew little about appliqué, the designs at first appeared overwhelming. But Jane's instruction and the rich experience of my classmates inspired me to complete the quilt. It was machine quilted by Barbara Persing.

—*Takako Yokoyama of Pottstown, Pennsylvania*

Tropical Twilight
50" x 50"

Jane's delightful menagerie of birds, blossoms, and butterflies sparked my imagination, and out came my very first art quilt. It all came together in a fiery landscape, as if one were peering through tropical foliage as evening begins. Once again, Jane has designed a collection of blocks that come alive with emotion and a peaceful tranquility.

—Monteen Bard of Carlisle, Pennsylvania

Winged Victory
53" x 53"

Just as winged creatures look beautiful in the air, butterflies and birds are beautiful in a quilt. After finishing this project, I felt a sense of soaring freedom. I want to thank Jane for her innovative techniques, boundless creativity, artistic color styling, and constant encouragement. Thanks also to Janice Hairston for her exquisite quilting and respect for my deadline.

—Gayle Lynn Rosenbach of Springfield, New Jersey

Fine Feathered Friends
46" x 46"

I loved the challenge of working on these detailed birds. Jane's approach to appliqué is to make the most complicated-looking block fun and easy to accomplish. Following her color-blending techniques resulted in effective shading and highlights, for a realistic look. I used mainly batik fabrics because of their tremendous range of shading within each color.

—Kim Jacobs of Chester Springs, Pennsylvania

In the Shadow of His Wings
43½" x 43½"

I love learning new techniques, such as Jane's famous sharp-point method and her tricks for making sheer wings with no visible seam allowances. Each creation reminds me that God is the creator of all things great and small, and he will keep me safe in the shadow of his wings. My thanks to Jane for her patience and for sharing her love of appliqué.

—*Peggy Heverin of Elkton, Maryland*

Moonlit Wings
50" x 50"

For the insect wings in the Dragonfly block and the Damsel Moth block, I used two layers of sheer fabric to achieve the desired shade. For the Cardinal block, I embroidered the evergreen branches. It was interesting to use Jane's color-blending technique and then reverse appliqué over it, which I did in the Forrester Butterfly block. Learning these techniques has opened up a whole new world of appliqué.

—Dot Rauscher of Roslyn, Pennsylvania

Wings Paired
40" x 48" (above)

My challenge for this quilt was to experiment with a dark background, which provided a wonderful opportunity to also work with pastel fabrics. I modified Jane's beautiful designs by either expanding the subject or combining elements from different blocks. As always, embellishing is half the fun! The border is a fiesta of cheerful ribbon and tiny glass beads.

—Diana Lynn Channer of Schwenksville, Pennsylvania

Seventeen
15" x 17" (right)

This hand-quilted wall hanging was coincidentally timed with the massive hatch of the seventeen-year cicada moth in the summer of 2004. I made the wings appear shimmery and translucent over the leaves by using the sheer-fabric layering technique introduced by Jane.

—Kim Jacobs of Chester Springs, Pennsylvania

Three Birds Take the Air
36" x 48½"

Making these birds was surprisingly easy! Setting my three favorite blocks into a quilt was a challenge. I used greens, blues, and purples to pull the colors in the birds together, with red as the accent color. Then I moved the blocks around many times to find the best way to showcase the birds.

—Laura J. Grams of Pennsburg, Pennsylvania

Nature's Beauties
46" x 46"

While working on these lovely blocks, I thought of the fun our Creator had designing these beautiful creatures. My thanks to Jane for her wonderful interpretation of them. They were truly a joy to stitch. The quilt was machine quilted by Carol Heisler of Lorac Designs in East Norriton, Pennsylvania.

—Dorothy W. Murdoch of West Chester, Pennsylvania

Wings in the Night
17" x 17"

I first met Jane when she spoke at my guild two years ago. I knew I wanted to improve my needle-turn appliqué with her innovative techniques. Jane liberated me from thinking all leaves should be green, and I applied that concept in this piece. The use of sheer-fabric overlays and glowing color combinations gives luminosity to this wall hanging.

—Kim Jacobs of Eleuthera, Bahamas

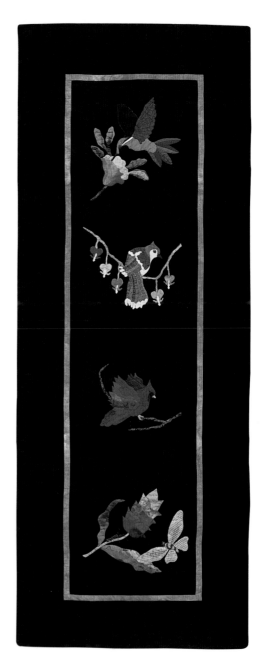

Bird-of-Paradise
23" x 48"

I found the task of naming this quilt a daunting one. Jane's designs deserve a very special title. While showing this quilt to my class of kindergartners at vacation Bible school, five-year-old Tyler shouted out, "I know, Bird-of-Paradise!" and so it is.

—Kathy DeCarli of Downingtown, Pennsylvania

Quilted Wings
36" x 36"

This quilt has been very satisfying for me. Reading the comments in Jane's previous book, Color-Blend Appliqué, *encouraged me to try Jane's class, and now I can't miss it! After hanging this quilt in my sewing room, I knew it was something special when my husband said, "Honey, your quilt is beautiful!"*

—Lisa White Reber of Red Hill, Pennsylvania

Monarch Out of Season

24" x 24"

I made this quilt to fulfill my guild challenge for 2003–2004. We had to make a quilt less than 30" per side, in autumn colors with prairie points. I found the beads for the body the minute that I walked into a bead shop. It was meant to be! The quilt name came from my husband informing me that butterflies don't fly in the autumn. I combined hand and machine quilting to enhance various parts of this piece.

—Carol Reen of Perkasie, Pennsylvania

Christmas Cardinal

40" x 40"

I love Jane's classes and the positive feelings she passes on to all of us. For this setting, I used Deborah J. Moffett-Hall's Cardinal Feathered Star pattern from Merry Christmas Quilts *(Martingale & Company, 2005), and I chose colors with a Christmas theme in mind. I love shades of teal, so I used those instead of true green, and I quilted holly shapes to keep the feel of winter throughout the quilt.*

—Carol Reen of Perkasie, Pennsylvania

There's a Bug in My Window
18" x 36"

Reverse appliqué with transparent, textured fabrics gave the wings of the Damsel moth a lacy look. Jane's technique for the stems also resulted in a realistic image. I chose a Cathedral Window setting, which my friend Gay Morales helped me finish by the due date. Aren't friends great?

—Jo Osborne Tate of Sterling, Virginia. Made with help from Veretha Gay Morales of East Brunswick, New Jersey.

Butterflies Are Free
21" x 25"

This project came from one of my early classes with Jane Townswick. I enjoy each of her patterns, but I really wasn't there long enough to do a whole quilt so I decided to work with one pattern at a time. Jane is such a wonderful, creative teacher, encouraging each and every one of us to think outside the box.

—Claudia M. Houtz of Tamaqua, Pennsylvania

Garden Wonders

22" x 38"

My thought for this quilt was to include three different patterns, showing how you can create a real art piece with Jane Townswick's designs. I truly enjoyed every aspect of this quilt, particularly the appliqué and the quilting. I love combining appliqué and quilting, and I really am inspired by all that Jane does.

—*Claudia M. Houtz of Tamaqua, Pennsylvania*

Gallery of Blocks

All of the blocks in this book measure 9" square finished (or 9½" square with seam allowances) and are intended to be set straight. If you wish to make your blocks larger or set the designs on point, you will need to adjust the size of the background fabric(s) accordingly.

The Birds

Hummingbird
Page 46

Cockatoo
Page 52

Cardinal
Page 57

Painted Bunting
Page 64

Marvelous Spatuletail
Page 71

Blue Jay
Page 78

The Butterflies and Moths

Dragonfly
Page 86

Damsel Moth
Page 92

Luna Moth
Page 97

Cicada Moth
Page 105

Forrester Butterfly
Page 112

Monarch Butterfly
Page 120

The Birds

Each of the six bird blocks in this book features a supply list indicating the fabrics I used to make that block; you may follow these lists, or let your own color preferences have free rein. Who says that a cardinal has to be red, or a painted bunting blue and orange?

Hummingbird

Gentle browns, beiges, and iridescent greens are typical of a Rufous hummingbird. Feel free to interpret this bird in the brighter greens and reds of its ruby-throated cousin, or use any colors that appeal to you.

Techniques

Color blending

Unit appliqué

Creating three-dimensionality with value

Steep points

Tiny circles

Inking

Fabrics and Supplies

- 11" square of fabric for background
- 6" square of fabric for fronts of leaves
- 6" square of fabric for backs of leaves
- Assorted scrap fabrics for wings, body, and tail feathers★
- 2 scraps of medium and dark fabrics for eye
- Assorted scrap fabrics for flower
- White gel roller pen
- Circle stencil
- Clear nail polish

★Use a range of values, including darker ones, for the back wing.

Stitching the Wings

1. Trace the front wing pattern from page 51 onto freezer paper, including the numbers and hatch marks that indicate where each feather touches the next. Cut along the outlines of the wing.

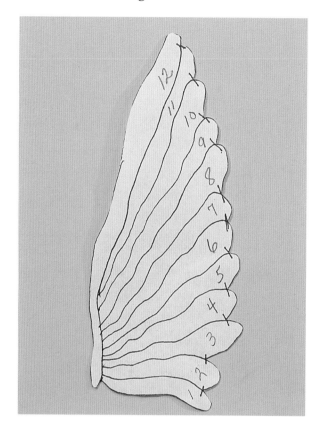

2. Cut feather shape 1 from the freezer-paper pattern and press it onto the right side of the fabric for this shape. Mark around the edges of the shape. Also make a hatch mark that aligns with the one on the template. Remove the freezer-paper template and cut the feather shape out with a ³⁄₁₆" seam allowance.

3. Clip the seam allowance up to the marked turning line at the hatch mark on feather shape 1. Starting at the clip, turn under the seam allowance of feather shape 1 and stitch it to a piece of fabric for feather shape 2.

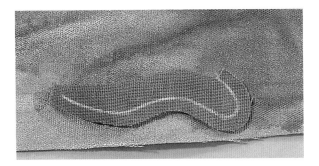

4. Cut feather shape 2 from the freezer-paper pattern and press it next to the stitched seam, as shown. Mark around the template, including the hatch mark, as in step 2.

5. Remove the freezer-paper template and cut a ³⁄₁₆" seam allowance around feather shape 2, taking care to cut away the excess fabric under shape 1 along the turned-under seam allowance of shape 1. Clip the seam allowance up to the marked turning line at the hatch mark on feather shape 2 and stitch it to a piece of fabric for feather shape 3.

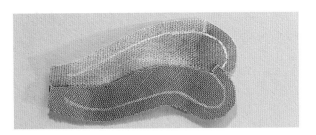

6. Repeat steps 3–5 to join feather shapes 3 through 12 in the same manner. Press the completed front wing unit.

7. For the back wing, repeat steps 2–5 to join feather shapes 1 through 6. Use slightly darker fabrics than for the front wing to add dimension. Press the completed back wing unit.

Stitching the Body

1. Trace the body pattern from page 51 onto freezer paper, continuing the line along the bird's back. Trace all hatch marks. Cut out the body pattern along the outlines.

2. Cut the head and throat shapes from the freezer-paper pattern. Press the head template onto the right side of the fabric for this shape and mark around it. Remove the freezer-paper template and cut a ³⁄₁₆" seam allowance around the head shape. Clip the seam allowance up to the marked turning line at the hatch mark shared with the throat shape. Starting at the clip, turn under the seam allowance of the head and stitch it to a piece of fabric for the throat shape.

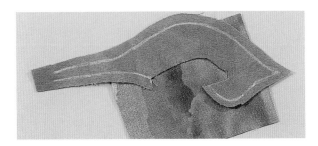

3. Press the throat template next to the stitched seam and mark around it. Remove the freezer-paper template and cut a ³⁄₁₆" seam allowance around the throat area. Clip the seam allowance up to the marked turning line at the hatch mark shared with the body shape. Starting at the clip, turn under the seam allowance of the throat and stitch it to a piece of fabric for the body shape.

4. Press the body template next to the stitched seam and mark around it. Remove the freezer-paper template and cut a ³⁄₁₆" seam allowance around the body.

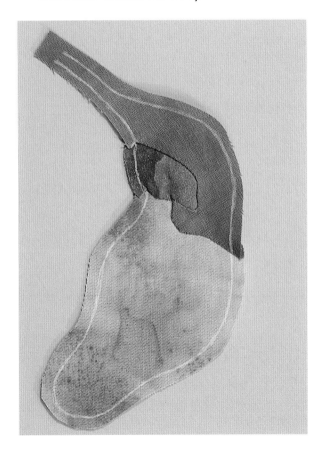

Stitching the Tail Feathers

1. Cut two 1½" x 6" strips of fabric for each tail feather. Make four sets. With right sides together, machine stitch or piece by hand the long edges of the strips together with a scant ¼" seam allowance. Press the seam allowance toward fabric 2, as indicated on the tail feather pattern on page 51.

2. Trace each of the tail feather patterns from page 51 onto freezer paper, drawing each end to a point and marking the center line. Cut the tail-feather shapes out on the outer marked lines and press them onto the right sides of the joined strips of fabric from step 1. Match the marked center line with the seam. Mark around each shape. Remove the freezer-paper template and cut a ³⁄₁₆" seam allowance around each feather shape.

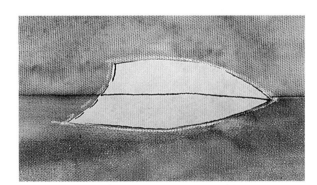

Stitching the Flower and Leaves

1. Referring to the photo on page 46 and "Stitching the Wings" on page 47, stitch the front and back flower units. Press the completed units.

2. In the same manner as step 1, stitch the four leaf units. Press the completed units.

Preparing the Stem

Trace the stem pattern from page 51 onto freezer paper and cut it out. Press the stem template onto the right sides of the stem fabric and mark around it. Remove the freezer-paper template and cut the stem out with a ³⁄₁₆" seam allowance.

Putting It All Together

1. Referring to the photo on page 46, arrange the stem, flower units, bird body, wings, tail feathers, and leaf units on the 11" background fabric square.

2. Stitch the units to the background fabric in the following order: the stem, the leaf units, the back flower unit, the tail feathers (refer to "Steep Points" on page 19), the back wing unit, the body unit, the front wing unit, and the front flower unit.

3. Using a circle stencil, mark a small circle on dark fabric for the eye (see pattern on page 51). Cut a ⅛" seam allowance around the circle. Stitch the circle onto a small piece of medium fabric, turning under just enough

of the seam allowance to take one stitch at a time. Mark a small leaf-like shape with two points around the stitched circle for the outer part of the eye. Cut a ⅛" seam allowance around this shape.

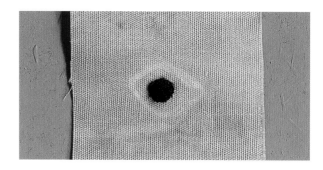

4. Referring to the photo on page 46, stitch the two-part eye to the bird's head. Using the white gel roller pen, add a highlight to the eye. Add a small drop of clear nail polish to seal the ink and keep it from smearing. Allow the nail polish to dry.

5. Press the completed block, referring to "Finishing" on page 16.

TOP OF BLOCK

Fabric #2

Fabric #1

12 11 10 9 8 7 6 5 4 3 2 1

6 5 4 3 2 1

Cockatoo

This fantasy-like bird reminded one of my students of Stravinsky's
L'oiseau du feu, or Firebird Suite. Its flowing feathers will give you a
chance to perfect your steep points.

Techniques

Color blending

Unit appliqué

Free-form branch and leaves

Steep points

Fabrics and Supplies

- 11" square of fabric for background
- Three 11" squares of fabric for branch
- Assorted scrap fabrics for body and wings
- Assorted scrap fabrics for leaves and top knot

The longest shape in the cockatoo takes a piece of fabric approximately 3" x 8".

Stitching the Branch and Leaves

1. Stitch the three-part free-form branch, referring to "Free-Form Stems and Branches" on page 18. Press the completed branch and stitch it onto the 11" background square, referring to the photo on page 52.

2. Cut 12 free-form leaves from scraps of fabric. Make sure to include a ³⁄₁₆" seam allowance around each leaf. Pin the cut leaves on the branch and set the background square aside until you finish stitching the units for the cockatoo.

Stitching the Bottom Wing Unit

1. Trace the bottom wing pattern from page 56 onto freezer paper, including the numbers and hatch marks that indicate where each feather touches the next. Cut along the outlines of the wing.

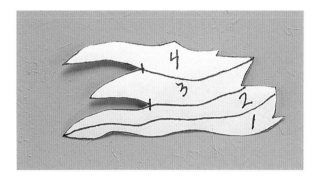

2. Cut feather shape 1 from the freezer-paper pattern and press it onto the right side of the fabric for this shape. Mark around the edges of the template. Also make a hatch mark that aligns with the one on the template. Remove the freezer-paper template and cut the feather shape out with a ³⁄₁₆" seam allowance.

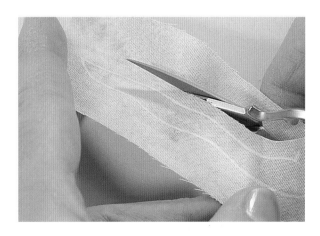

3. Clip the seam allowance up to the marked turning line at the hatch mark on feather shape 1. Starting at the clip, turn under the seam allowance of feather shape 1 and stitch it to a piece of fabric for feather shape 2.

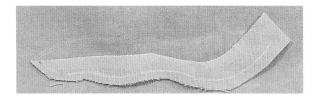

4. Cut feather shape 2 from the freezer-paper pattern and press it next to the stitched seam, as shown. Mark around the template, including the hatch mark, as in step 2.

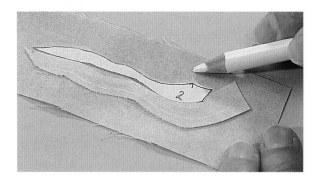

5. Remove the freezer-paper template and cut a ³⁄₁₆" seam allowance around feather shape 2, taking care to cut away the excess fabric under shape 1 along the turned-under seam allowance of shape 1. Clip the seam allowance up to the marked turning line at the hatch mark on feather shape 2. Starting at the clip, turn under the seam allowance of feather shape 2 and stitch it to a piece of fabric for feather shape 3.

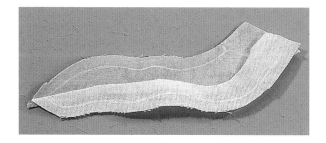

6. Repeat steps 3–5 to join feather shapes 3 through 5 in the same manner. Press the completed bottom wing unit.

Stitching the Middle and Top Wing Units

1. Referring to the photo on page 52 and "Stitching the Bottom Wing Unit" on page 53, stitch the four-part middle wing unit. Press.

2. Referring to "Stitching the Bottom Wing Unit" on page 53, stitch the three-part top wing unit. Press.

Stitching the Body and Top Knot

1. Trace the body and top knot from page 56 onto freezer paper, including the numbers and hatch marks that indicate where each piece touches the next. Cut along the outlines of the patterns.

2. Referring to "Stitching the Bottom Wing Unit" on page 53, stitch the body and top knot units. Press the completed units. Stitch the top of the bird's head to the top knot unit. Press.

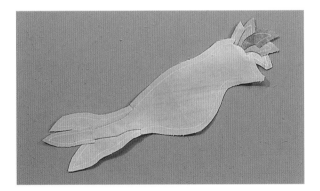

3. Press the claw shape onto the right side of the fabric for this shape. Mark around the edges of the template, including the hatch marks. Remove the freezer-paper template and cut the claw shape out with a ³⁄₁₆" seam allowance.

Putting It All Together

1. Arrange and pin each of the wing units, the body/top knot unit, and the claw on the stitched free-form branch. Refer to the photo on page 52.

2. Stitch the units to the background fabric in the following order: the claw, the body/top knot unit (refer to "Steep Points" on page 19), the bottom wing unit, the middle wing unit, and the top wing unit.

3. Stitch the free-form leaves on the branch. Press and trim the completed block, referring to "Finishing" on page 16.

TOP OF BRANCH

Cardinal

Although cardinals come in other colors, the red ones have always been my favorites.
Whatever colors you choose for this cardinal, include a range of values,
including medium and lighter ones for the front wing and darker ones
for the back wing to create the look of sunlight and shadow.

Techniques

Color blending

Unit appliqué

Free-form branches

Using value to create three-dimensionality

Steep points

Tiny circles

Inking

Fabrics and Supplies

- 11" square of fabric for background
- Two 11" squares of fabric for branch
- Assorted scrap fabrics for body, tail feathers, and wings*
- Scrap of black fabric for face and claw
- 2 scraps of yellow or gold fabric for beak
- 2 dark scraps of fabric for eye
- 3 (or more) Pigma permanent-marking pens in greens and browns
- Circle stencil
- White gel roller pen
- Clear nail polish

Include a range of values for the wings, from darks to mediums and lights.

Stitching the Branch

Stitch the two-part free-form branch, referring to "Free-Form Stems and Branches" on page 18 and the photo on page 57. Press the completed branch and stitch it onto the 11" background square. Set the background square aside until you finish stitching the bird units.

Stitching the Front Wing Unit

1. Trace the front wing pattern from page 63 onto freezer paper, except for feather shape 9; trace shape 9 separately from the others. As you trace each of the first eight feather shapes, extend the unpointed ends to allow some underlap for adding shape 9 later. Include the dashed lines, the numbers, and the hatch marks that indicate where each feather shape touches the next. Cut along the outlines of the front wing unit.

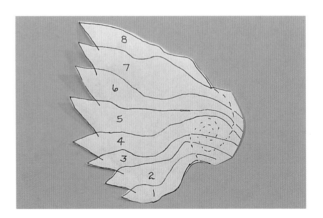

2. Cut feather shape 1 from the freezer-paper pattern and press it onto the right side of the fabric for this shape. Mark around the edges of the template. Also make a hatch

mark that aligns with the one on the template. Remove the freezer-paper template and cut the feather shape out with a ³⁄₁₆" seam allowance.

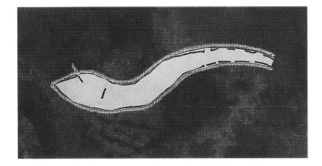

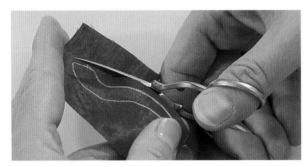

3. Clip the seam allowance up to the marked turning line at the hatch mark on feather shape 1. Starting at the clip, turn under the seam allowance of feather shape 1 and stitch it to a piece of fabric for feather shape 2.

4. Cut feather shape 2 from the freezer-paper pattern and press it next to the stitched seam, as shown. Mark around the template, including the hatch mark, as in step 2.

5. Remove the freezer-paper template and cut a ³⁄₁₆" seam allowance around feather shape 2, taking care to cut away the excess fabric under shape 1 along the turned-under seam allowance of shape 1. Clip the seam allowance up to the marked turning line at the hatch mark of feather shape 2. Starting at the clip, turn under the seam allowance of feather shape 2 and stitch it to a piece of fabric for feather shape 3.

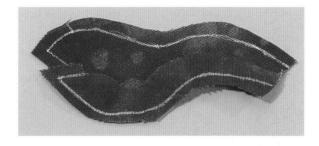

6. Repeat steps 3–5 to join feather shapes 3 through 8 in the same manner.

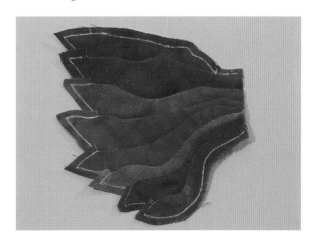

7. To add feather shape 9, start by stitching shape 8 to the fabric for shape 9, beginning at the dot and ending at the hatch mark (see pattern on page 63). Cut out the pattern for feather shape 9 and press it next to the stitched line. Mark around it. Remove the freezer-paper template and cut a ³⁄₁₆" seam allowance around shape 9, leaving the curved spiral area intact.

8. On the wrong side of your work, clip the seam allowance up to the stitched line, approximately ¼" from the point where you started stitching.

9. Using a bamboo skewer or toothpick, lift up the seam allowance beyond your stitching line.

10. Using your index finger, press down hard on the seam allowance to create a crisp fold.

11. Gently bring the unstitched portion of shape 9 to the right side of your work, overlapping the first eight shapes, as shown.

12. Referring to the photo on page 57, stitch the entire remaining portion of shape 9 in place, covering the unpointed edges of the first eight feather shapes. Trim the excess fabric of the first eight shapes underneath shape 9. Press the completed front wing unit.

Stitching the Back Wing and Tail Feather Units

1. Referring to the photo on page 57 and "Stitching the Front Wing Unit" on page 58, stitch the back wing unit. Follow the numbers on the pattern on page 63. Press the completed back wing unit.

2. Referring to the photo on page 57 and "Stitching the Front Wing Unit" on page 58, stitch the tail feather unit. Follow the numbers on the pattern on page 63. Press the completed tail feather unit.

Stitching the Body Unit

1. Trace the body and claw patterns from page 63 onto freezer paper, rounding out the back of the body, as shown. Cut the patterns out on the marked lines. Press the claw shape onto the right side of the fabric for this shape. Mark around the edges of the template, including the hatch marks. Remove the freezer-paper template and cut the claw shape out with a ³⁄₁₆" seam allowance.

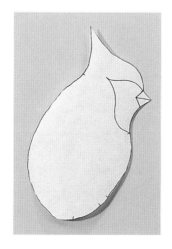

2. Cut the face-and-beak shape from the body freezer-paper pattern. Then press the remaining body template onto the right side of the fabric for the body and mark around it. Remove the freezer-paper template and cut a ³⁄₁₆" seam allowance around the body.

3. Stitch the bird's body to a piece of fabric for the face, as shown. Cut the beak from the face-and-beak template. Press the face template next to your stitched line and mark around it. Remove the freezer-paper template and cut a ³⁄₁₆" seam allowance around the face. Trim the excess face fabric underneath the bird body.

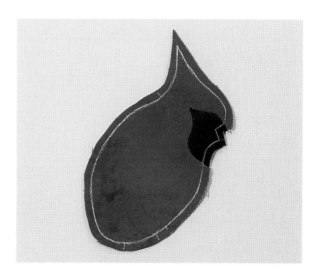

4. Fold a ³⁄₁₆" seam allowance in a small scrap of yellow fabric for the beak. Stitch the folded edge to the right side of a second piece of yellow fabric. Stitch the beak opening of the face to the yellow beak unit, aligning the stitching line on the yellow beak fabric with the inner angle of the beak opening on the face. To create the beak, press the beak template at the beak opening on the face and mark two short, straight lines from the edges of the beak opening to the stitched line.

5. Cut a ³⁄₁₆" seam allowance around the marked beak shape, trimming away the excess beak fabric from underneath the face.

Putting It All Together

1. Using the Pigma pens and referring to the photo on page 57, mark free-form pine needles along the branch on the background square. Be relaxed and have fun—there is no wrong way to mark the pine needles. They can go any direction and look great.

2. Arrange and pin the bird units on the background square as desired.

3. Stitch the units to the branch on the background square in the following order: the claw, the tail feather unit, the back wing unit, the body unit, and the front wing unit. Refer to "Steep Points" on page 19 for all points on the wings, head, and beak.

4. Using a circle stencil, mark a small circle for the eye on a dark fabric. Cut a ¹⁄₈" seam allowance around the circle. Stitch the circle onto another small piece of dark fabric, turning just enough of the seam allowance to take one stitch at a time. Cut a slightly larger circle around the first stitched circle.

5. Referring to the photo on page 57, stitch the two-part eye to the bird's face. Using a white gel roller pen, add a highlight to the eye. Add a small drop of clear nail polish to seal the ink and keep it from smearing. Allow the nail polish to dry.

6. Press and trim the completed block, referring to "Finishing" on page 16.

Painted Bunting

*Gilded branches and leaves make a shiny perch for this colorful bunting.
If you like the idea of using lamé, consider one of the new cotton lamés
now available in rainbow colors.*

Techniques

Color blending

Unit appliqué

Edging shapes with narrow bands of color

Working with specialty fabrics: silk douppioni and tissue lamé

Tiny circles

Inking

Fabrics and Supplies

- 11" square of fabric for background
- 11" square of fabric for branch
- 11" square of tissue or cotton lamé for branch and leaves
- Assorted scrap fabrics for leaves
- Assorted scrap fabrics for body, beak, feathers, eye, and claw
- 3" square of silk douppioni or cotton fabric for shoulder piece
- 3" square of lightweight, fusible tricot interfacing (for silk douppioni only)
- 11" square of lightweight, fusible tricot interfacing (for both lamé and silk douppioni)
- Circle stencil
- Cotton press cloth
- Template plastic (for leaves only)
- Sharpie permanent pen
- White gel roller pen
- Clear nail polish

Stitching the Branch

1. Place the 11" square of lightweight, fusible tricot interfacing on top of the wrong side of the tissue or cotton lamé. Place the cotton press cloth over the fusible interfacing and press the interfacing to the lamé to strengthen it and make it easier to handle during the stitching process.

2. Stitch the three-part free-form branch onto the 11" background square, referring to "Free-Form Stems and Branches" on page 18 and the photo on page 64. Use the fabric from step 1 and the 11" square of branch fabric. Place the cotton press cloth on top of the background square and press. Set the background square aside until you finish stitching the bird units.

Accenting the Leaves with Lamé

1. To make a leaf with lamé along the edge, trace one of the leaf patterns from page 70 onto template plastic and cut it out. (Cutting a template from plastic rather than freezer paper will allow you use the template more than once to make identical leaves.) Mark around the leaf template on the right side of a scrap of leaf fabric and cut out a leaf with a ³⁄₁₆" seam allowance.

2. Starting and ending approximately ¼" in from the points, stitch one side of the leaf to the interfaced lamé. Using sharp scissors, trim the lamé to ¼" from your stitched line;

make sure to cut the fabric beyond your stitched line at each end, and trim the excess lamé underneath the leaf. Repeat for one more leaf.

3. To make a leaf with lamé down the center, trace the half-leaf pattern from page 70 onto template plastic and cut it out. Mark around the template on the right side of a scrap of leaf fabric; repeat with a second scrap of leaf fabric. Cut them out with a ³⁄₁₆" seam allowance.

4. Stitch the straight edge of each half-leaf to the interfaced lamé, exposing a tiny bit of lamé between the two edges. The edges should meet at the points of the leaf. Trim away the excess lamé underneath the leaf.

5. Using the leaf template from step 1, mark and cut seven more leaves from the scrap leaf fabrics; use a ³⁄₁₆" seam allowance.

Stitching the Wing Units and Tail Feathers

1. Trace the left wing unit pattern from page 70 onto freezer paper, including the numbers and hatch marks that indicate where each feather touches the next. Cut along the outlines of the wing unit.

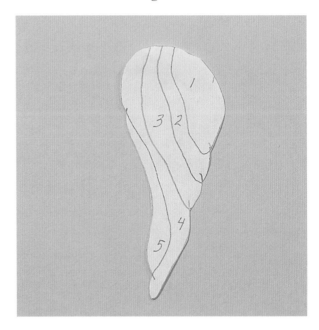

2. Cut feather shape 1 from the pattern and press it onto the right side of the fabric for shape 1. Mark around the template. Also make hatch marks on the fabric that align with the ones on the template. Remove the freezer-paper template and cut feather shape 1 out with a ³⁄₁₆" seam allowance.

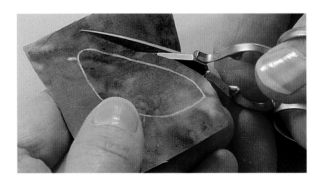

3. Clip the seam allowance up to the marked turning line at the hatch marks on feather shape 1. Starting at a clip, turn under the seam allowance of feather shape 1 between the clips. Stitch it to a piece of fabric for feather shape 2.

4. Cut feather shape 2 from the freezer-paper pattern and press it next to the stitched seam on shape 1, as shown. Mark around the template, including the hatch mark, as in step 2.

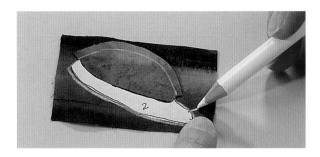

5. Remove the freezer-paper template and cut a ³⁄₁₆" seam allowance around feather shape 2, taking care to cut away the excess fabric under shape 1 along the turned-under seam allowance of shape 1. Clip the seam allowance up to the marked turning line at the

hatch mark of feather shape 2. Starting at the clip, turn under the seam allowance of feather shape 2. Stitch it to a piece of fabric for feather shape 3.

6. Repeat steps 3–5 to join feather shapes 3 through 5 in the same manner. Press the completed left wing unit.

7. In the same manner as the left wing unit, stitch the right wing unit and the tail feather unit, referring to the photo on page 64.

Stitching the Head and Body

1. Trace the head-and-body, beak, shoulder, and claw pattern shapes from page 70 onto freezer paper. Round out the head-and-body shape to provide underlap for the wing units, and cut it out. Trace the shoulder pattern separately and cut it out. Cut the claw pattern out. Press the claw shape onto the right side of the fabric for the claw. Mark around the edges of the template, including the hatch marks. Remove the freezer-paper template and cut the claw shape from the fabric with a ³⁄₁₆" seam allowance.

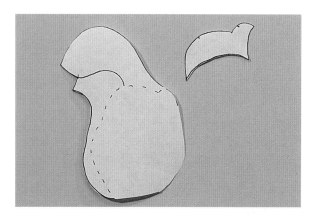

2. Cut the head shape from the head-and-body pattern. Press it to the right side of the fabric for the head and mark around it, including the hatch marks. Remove the freezer-paper template and cut a ³⁄₁₆" seam allowance around the head shape. Stitch it to the fabric for the body. Press the body template next to the stitched line and mark around it. Cut a ³⁄₁₆" seam allowance around the body.

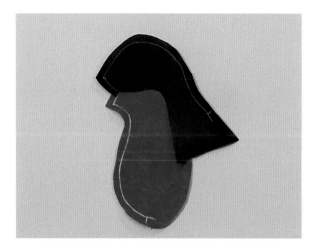

3. Press the shoulder template onto the right side of the shoulder fabric and mark around it, including the hatch marks. Note that if you use silk douppioni for the shoulder piece, as I did, you will need to press fusible interfacing to the wrong side of the fabric for stability. Remove the freezer-paper

template and cut the shoulder piece out with a ³⁄₁₆" seam allowance. Stitch the shoulder piece to the head-and-body unit, matching the hatch marks.

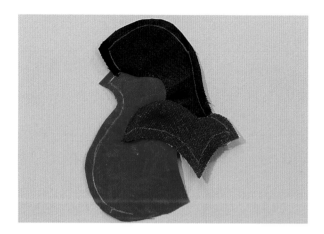

4. Cut the beak pattern apart. Press the top beak onto the right side of the beak fabric and mark around it. Also make a hatch mark that aligns with the one on the template. Remove the freezer-paper template and cut the top beak out with a ³⁄₁₆" seam allowance. Clip the seam allowance at the hatch mark. Starting at the clip, stitch the top beak to the fabric for the bottom beak.

Either press the bottom beak template next to the stitched line and mark around it, or simply draw a short, curved line for the bottom of the beak. Stitch the head to the beak.

Putting It All Together

1. Arrange and pin the bird units and leaves onto the background square, referring to the photo on page 64.

2. Stitch the units to the background square in the following order: the claw, the tail feather unit, the head-and-body unit, the left and right wing units, and the leaves.

3. Using a circle stencil, mark a small circle for the eye on a dark fabric. Cut a ⅛" seam allowance around the circle. Stitch the circle onto another small piece of dark fabric, turning under just enough of the seam allowance to take one stitch at a time. Cut a slightly larger circle around the stitched circle.

4. Referring to the photo on page 64, stitch the two-part eye to the bird's face. Using a white gel roller pen, add a highlight to the eye. Add a small drop of clear nail polish to seal the ink and keep it from smearing. Allow the nail polish to dry.

5. Using a cotton press cloth and referring to "Finishing" on page 16, press and trim the completed block.

TOP OF BLOCK

Marvelous Spatuletail

Exotic birds are filled with beautiful hues and shapes. Check your local stitchery shops for decorative braids and colorful cotton lamés that will make the wings of this Peruvian hummingbird shimmer with light.

Techniques

Color blending

Unit appliqué

Working with specialty fabrics: cotton lamé

Steep points

Tiny circles

Inking

Fabrics and Supplies

- 11" square of fabric for background
- 4" x 8" rectangle of fabric for body shape 3
- Assorted 6" squares of cotton lamé for shoulder piece and wings
- Assorted scrap fabrics for body, head, wings, beak, eye, and tail feathers
- 6" squares of lightweight, fusible tricot interfacing (for cotton lamé)
- 8" length of narrow decorative braid for tail feathers (I used 1⁄16"-wide braid)
- Cotton press cloth
- Circle stencil
- Black permanent marking pen
- White gel roller pen
- Clear nail polish

Stitching the Wing Units

1. Trace the left wing pattern from page 77 onto freezer paper, including the numbers and hatch marks. Cut along the outlines of the wing unit.

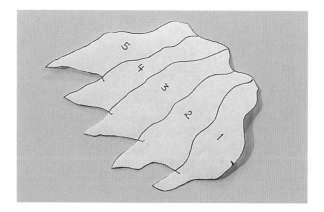

2. Cut feather shape 1 from the pattern and press it onto the right side of the fabric for this shape. Mark around the template. Also make hatch marks that align with the ones on the template. Remove the freezer-paper template and cut feather shape 1 out with a 3⁄16" seam allowance. Clip the seam allowance at the hatch mark between shapes 1 and 2 as shown.

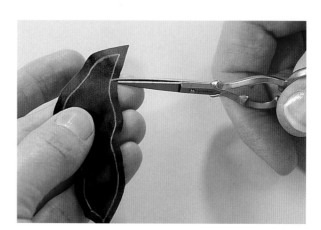

3. For stability, press the squares of lightweight, fusible tricot interfacing to the wrong sides of the cotton lamé squares by using the cotton press cloth and an iron set at the cotton setting.

4. Stitch feather shape 1 to a square of interfaced cotton lamé, ending at the clip. Trim the cotton lamé to approximately ¼" from the stitched line, and ¼" beyond the point where you stopped stitching. Also trim the excess cotton lamé underneath feather shape 1.

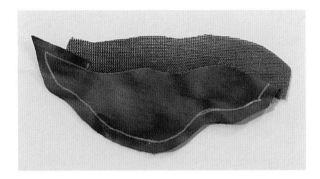

5. Turn under an uneven seam allowance along the long edge of the cotton lamé and stitch it to a piece of fabric for feather shape 2.

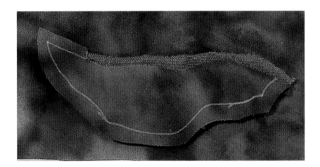

6. Cut feather shape 2 from the pattern. Press it next to the stitched edge of feather shape 1 and *on top* of the cotton lamé piece. Mark around feather shape 2, including the hatch mark as shown.

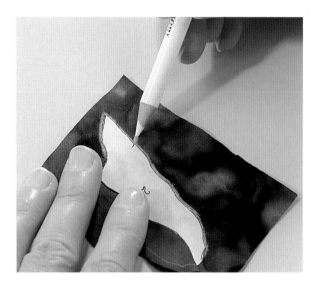

7. Remove the freezer-paper template and cut out feather shape 2 with a ³⁄₁₆" seam allowance as shown. Clip the seam allowance at the hatch mark between shapes 2 and 3.

8. Repeat steps 4–7 to add feather shapes 2 through 5 and the uneven lamé shapes between them, referring to the photo on page 71.

9. Stitch the right wing unit in the same manner as the left wing unit.

Stitching the Body Unit

1. Trace the body pattern from page 77 onto freezer paper.

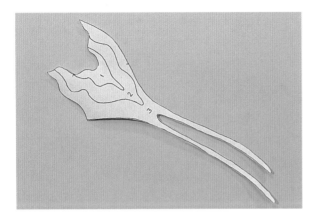

2. Cut body shape 1 from the pattern and press it onto the right side of the fabric for this shape. Mark around the template, remove it, and cut out body shape 1 with a ³⁄₁₆" seam allowance. Stitch body shape 1 to a piece of fabric for body shape 2.

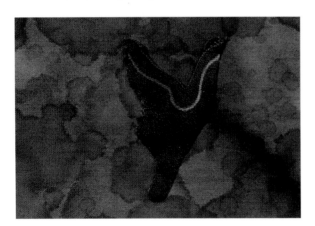

3. Cut body shape 2 from the pattern and press it next to the stitched line. Mark around the template. Remove the freezer-paper template and cut a ³⁄₁₆" seam allowance around body shape 2.

4. Stitch body shape 2 to the 4" x 8" rectangle of fabric for body shape 3. Press the template for body shape 3 next to the stitched line and mark around it, including the hatch mark. Remove the freezer-paper template and cut a ³⁄₁₆" seam allowance except between the long, narrow feathers.

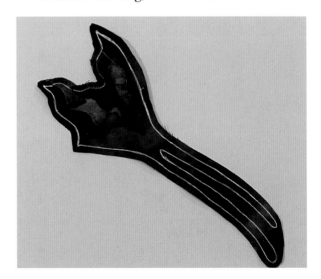

Stitching the Head Unit

1. Trace and cut the freezer-paper pattern for the head unit. Referring to "Stitching the Body Unit" on page 74, stitch the eight-part head unit in the same manner.

2. Stitch the bird's head to a piece of fabric for the beak. Press the beak template next to the stitched line and mark around it. Remove the freezer-paper template and cut a ³⁄₁₆" seam allowance around the beak.

3. Trace the shoulder pattern onto freezer paper and cut it out. Press it onto the right side of the fabric for this shape. Mark around the template, remove it, and cut out the shoulder shape with a ³⁄₁₆" seam allow-ance. Set it aside until you are ready to assemble the pieces.

Stitching the Spatuletail Feathers

1. Trace the left spatuletail pattern from page 77 onto freezer paper and cut it along the outlines of the tail. Cut shape 1 from the pattern.

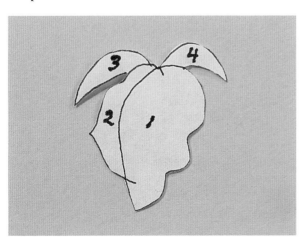

2. Press the shape 1 template onto the right side of the fabric for shape 1. Mark around it. Also make hatch marks that align with the ones on the template. Remove the freezer-paper template and cut out shape 1 with a ³⁄₁₆" seam allowance. Clip the seam allowance at the hatch marks between shapes 1 and 2. Starting and ending at the clips, stitch shape 1 to a piece of fabric for shape 2.

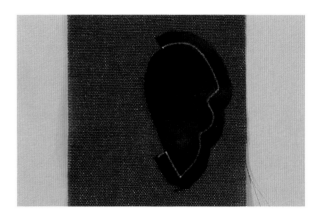

3. Cut shape 2 from the pattern and press it next to the stitched line on shape 1. Mark around the template, including the hatch mark. Remove the template and cut a ³⁄₁₆" seam allowance around shape 2, and then trim away the excess fabric underneath shape 1. Clip the seam allowance at the hatch mark between shapes 2 and 3. Starting at the clip, stitch shape 2 to a piece of fabric for shape 3.

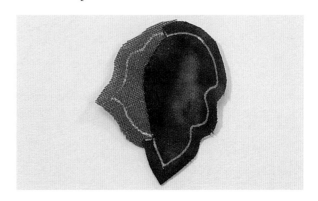

4. In the same manner as shape 2, add shapes 3 and 4.

5. Repeat steps 1–4 for the right spatuletail feather.

Putting It All Together

1. Stitch the body to the wing units, referring to the photo on page 71.

2. Stitch the lower edge of the shoulder piece to the body-and-wing unit.

3. Stitch the top edge of the shoulder unit to the head unit.

4. Pin the bird to the background square, referring to the photo on page 71. Position and pin the tail feathers near the long, narrow feathers of the body, as desired.

5. Stitch the two lengths of decorative braid to the background square, starting underneath the two long, narrow feathers and ending underneath the tail feathers.

6. Stitch the bird unit to the background square, referring to the photo on page 71 and to "Steep Points" on page 19. As you stitch the long, narrow feathers, stitch the outer edges first; then cut between them and stitch the inner edges.

7. Using a circle stencil, mark a small circle on the fabric for the eye. Cut the circle out with a ⅛" seam allowance. Stitch the eye to the bird's head, referring to the photo on page 71. Using a black permanent marking pen, enhance the size of the eye by drawing a narrow, black outline around the eye. Finish by using a white gel roller pen to add a highlight to the eye. Add a drop of clear nail polish to the highlight to seal the ink and keep it from smearing. Allow the nail polish to dry.

8. Press and trim the completed block, referring to "Finishing" on page 16.

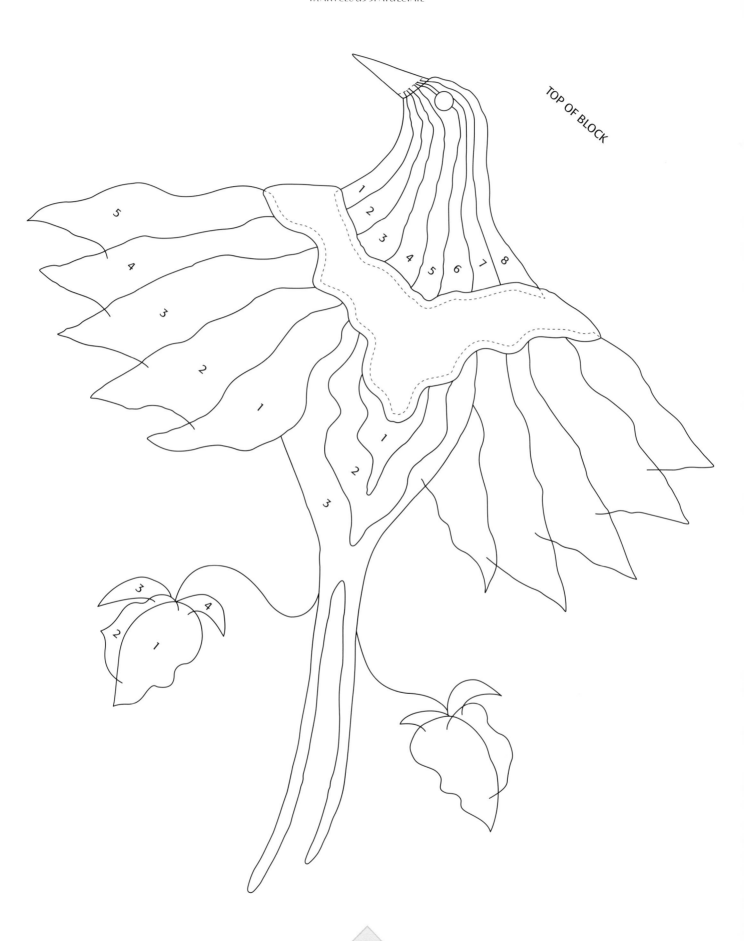

TOP OF BLOCK

Blue Jay

Combine dark and medium purples, blues, and bluish greens to stitch this little blue jay, or lighten him up with brighter hues in the same color family. You can give the wings and tail feathers a blended look by inking narrow, random zigzags across each feather fabric with a permanent fabric pen.

Techniques

Color blending

Unit appliqué

Free-form branches

Edging shapes with narrow bands of color

Steep points

Tiny circles

Inking

Fabrics and Supplies

- 11" square of fabric for background

- Two 11" squares of fabric for branch and stems

- Assorted medium and dark scrap fabrics for body, head, eye, beak, wings, and tail feathers

- Assorted light scrap fabrics for wings, and tail feathers

- Assorted bright, medium, and light scrap fabrics for bleeding hearts

- Pigma black permanent marking pen

- Circle stencil

- White gel roller pen

- Clear nail polish

Stitching the Branch and Bleeding Hearts

1. Stitch the two-part free-form branch with five stems, referring to "Free-Form Stems and Branches" on page 18. Press the completed branch with stems and stitch it onto the background square, referring to the photo on page 78.

2. Trace a bleeding-heart pattern from page 84 onto freezer paper, including the hatch marks, and cut it out. Cut the flower tip from the pattern and lay it aside. Press the remaining bleeding-heart template onto the right side of a fabric for a bleeding heart and trace around it, marking the fabric at each of the six hatch marks. Remove the freezer-paper template and cut a ³⁄₁₆" seam allowance around the bleeding heart, except at the deep inner curve at the bottom edge of the shape.

3. Clip the fabric at the hatch marks on one side of the bleeding heart. Stitch the outer curve of the bleeding heart to a contrast fabric, starting and ending at the clips. Cut the fabric to ¼" from your stitched line, adding ⅛" at each end of the seam.

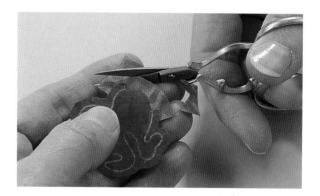

4. Repeat step 3 for the opposite outer curve of the bleeding heart.

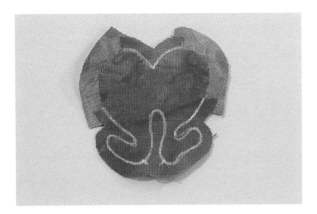

5. Clip the seam allowance at the hatch marks along the lower edge of the bleeding heart. Cut and stitch the deep inner curve to a piece of fabric for the flower tip, beginning and ending at the clips. Press the flower-tip template next to the stitched line and mark around it. Remove the freezer-paper template and cut a ³⁄₁₆" seam allowance around the flower tip.

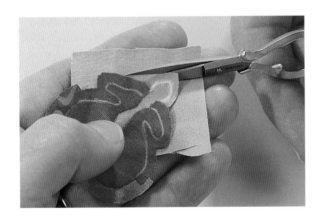

6. Repeat steps 4–6 for the remaining four bleeding hearts.

Stitching the Head-and-Body Unit

1. Trace the head and body from the pattern on page 84 onto freezer paper, extending the body shape so that it will underlap the wings.

2. Cut the back and top head pieces apart and press them onto the right side of the fabric for the shapes. Mark around them, remove them from the fabric, and cut a ³⁄₁₆" seam allowance around them. Stitch the two head pieces together.

3. Stitch the inner curve of the head unit to the fabric for the body, stopping at the inner point of the beak. Press the freezer-paper body template next to the stitched line and mark around it. Remove the freezer-paper template and cut a ³⁄₁₆" seam allowance around the body.

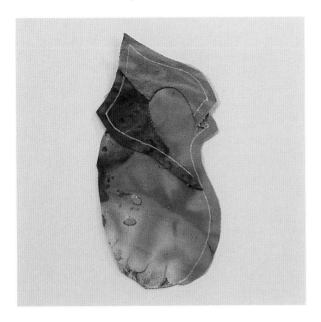

4. Referring to the photo on page 78, stitch the beak opening on the head unit to a piece of fabric for the beak. Press the beak template next to the stitched line and mark around it. Remove the freezer-paper template and cut a ³⁄₁₆" seam allowance around the beak. Press the completed head-and-body unit.

Stitching the Wing Unit

1. Trace the wing unit pattern from page 84 onto freezer paper, including the numbers, and cut it out.

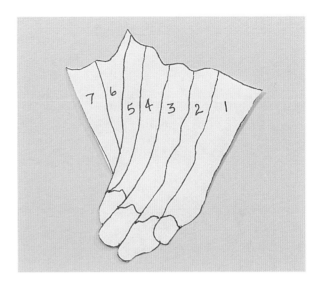

2. Cut feather shape 1 from the pattern. Cut the tip shape from the feather shape and press it onto the right side of a light fabric. Mark around the tip shape, remove it, and cut a ³⁄₁₆" seam allowance around it. Stitch the tip shape to a piece of fabric for feather shape 1. Press the template for feather shape 1 next to the stitched line and mark around it.

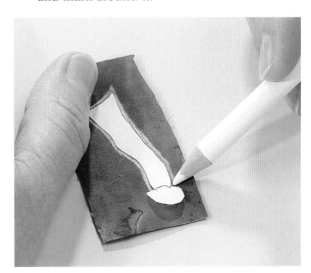

3. Remove the freezer-paper template and cut a ³⁄₁₆" seam allowance around feather shape 1 to complete the first feather unit.

4. Repeat step 2 for feather shape 2. Remove the freezer-paper template.

5. Stitch feather unit 1 from step 3 to the marked feather unit 2 from step 4.

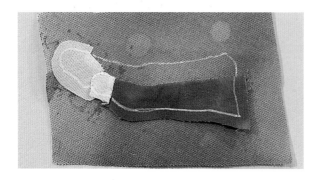

6. Cut a ³⁄₁₆" seam allowance around the marked feather unit 2.

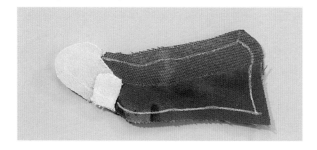

7. Repeat steps 4–6 to add the remaining feather units and shapes. Press the completed wing unit.

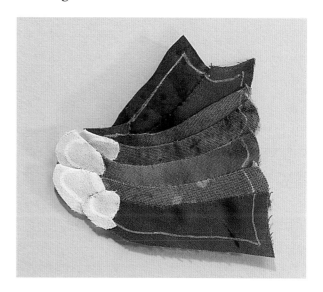

Stitching the Shoulder Unit

1. Trace the shoulder patterns from page 84 onto freezer paper and cut them out as a unit.

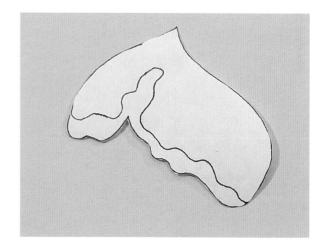

2. Cut the two shoulder shapes apart and press the top shoulder template onto the right side of the fabric for the shoulder. Mark around the template, remove it, and cut the shape out with a ³⁄₁₆" seam allowance. Leave the deep inner curved area intact. Stitch the top shoulder piece to a piece of light fabric for the bottom shoulder piece, clipping and stitching the deep inner curve when you reach it.

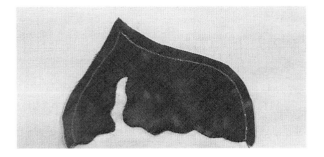

3. Press the freezer-paper template for the bottom shoulder piece next to the stitched line and mark around it. Remove the freezer-paper template and cut a ³⁄₁₆" seam allowance around the shape. Press the completed shoulder unit.

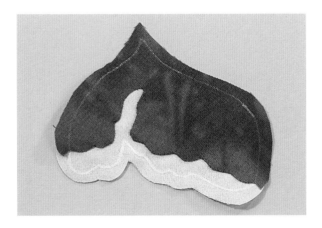

Stitching the Tail Feather Unit

Referring to "Stitching the Wing Unit" on page 81, stitch together the seven tail feather units. Press the completed tail feather unit.

Putting It All Together

1. Stitch the bleeding hearts to the stems on the background square, referring to the photo on page 78.

2. Stitch the bird units to the branch on the background square in the following order: the head-and-body unit (refer to "Steep Points" on page 19), the tail feather unit, the wing unit, and the shoulder unit.

3. Referring to the photo on page 78, use a circle template to mark and stitch a small circle and a medium circle together for the eye. Stitch the two-part eye to the bird's head. Using the white gel roller pen, add a highlight to the eye. Add a small drop of clear nail polish to seal the ink and keep it from smearing. Allow the nail polish to dry.

4. Using a black permanent marking pen, draw short, close zigzag lines across the stitched wings and tail feathers. Press and trim the completed block, referring to "Finishing" on page 16.

TOP OF BLOCK

The Butterflies and Moths

Each of the following butterfly blocks and moth blocks features a supply list indicating the fabrics I used to make the blocks. You can use the same colors I did, or let your imagination and creativity lead you into new territory.

Dragonfly

The idea of transparent appliqué intrigued me for a long time before this dragonfly came into being. I wanted to work with metallic sheer fabrics without letting any seam allowances show through them. The solution I came up with was a trompe l'oeil process that involved layering both regular and reverse appliqué.

Techniques

Color blending

Unit appliqué

Transparent appliqué

Reverse appliqué

Working with specialty fabrics:
   metallic sheers

Steep points

Fabrics and Supplies

- 11" square of fabric for background
- 6" x 11" piece of same background fabric as 11" square for area under wings
- 6" x 11" piece of see-through metallic sheer fabric for wings
- Assorted 9" squares of fabric for leaves
- Assorted scrap fabrics for body
- Cotton press cloth

Stitching the Leaves

Referring to "Starting to Stitch" on page 14, trace, cut, and stitch the five leaves to the 11" background square in the order numbered on the pattern pieces. Overlap and underlap the lower ends of the leaves, as shown, before stitching them in place.

Stitching the Wings

1. Trace the upper and lower dragonfly wing shapes from page 91 onto freezer paper and cut the templates out. Note that these shapes are traced as double wing shapes and not as individual wings. Mark lines on the templates to indicate where the wings overlap the leaves.

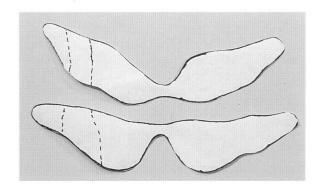

2. Press the dragonfly wing templates onto the background square, overlapping leaf 5 as shown. Mark around the wing templates and then remove the templates.

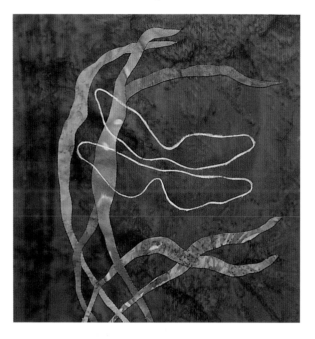

3. Cut a ³⁄₁₆" seam allowance *inside* the marked lines of the wing shapes. Lay the background square aside.

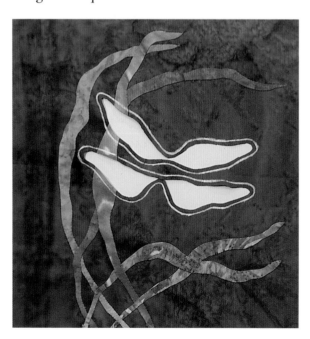

4. Using the pattern on page 91, trace the area of leaf 5 that falls between the dashed lines onto freezer paper and cut out a template for this partial leaf. Press the template onto the same fabric you used earlier for leaf 5 and mark around it. Remove the template and cut a ³⁄₁₆" seam allowance around the partial leaf shape. Stitch the leaf onto the 6" x 11" piece of background fabric 3½" from the left edge, as shown.

5. Place the 6" x 11" piece of metallic sheer fabric on top of the stitched partial leaf.

6. Place the background square with the cutout wing shapes from step 3 over the stitched partial leaf layered with metallic sheer fabric, aligning the edges of the partial leaf underneath with the edges of the leaf on the background square above. Pin the layers of fabric securely in place.

7. Referring to the photo on page 86, reverse appliqué the edges of the top layer of the wing shapes to the fabrics underneath, starting with the leaf areas that need to be in alignment and finishing with the remainder of the wing shapes. Place a press cloth over the stitched wing shapes and gently press the background square. Turn your work to the wrong side and trim the lower layers of fabric to ³⁄₁₆" from the stitched lines around the wing shapes.

Stitching the Body Unit

1. Trace the body shape marked with an X from page 91 onto freezer paper and cut the template out, or simply cut a free-form body shape that is approximately ³⁄₈" x ⁵⁄₈".

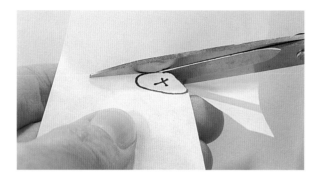

2. Press this body shape onto fabric that you selected for it. Mark around the template, remove it, and cut the shape out with a ³⁄₁₆" seam allowance. Stitch one side of this shape to a second piece of body fabric.

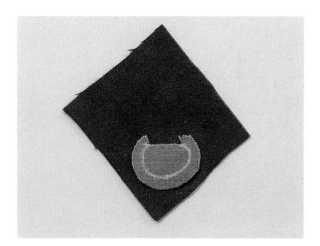

3. Using a small pair of embroidery scissors, cut out a second body piece by eye, approximately ¼" to ³⁄₈" from your stitched line to allow for seam allowances. The shape of each body piece will be more interesting if

you cut and stitch them free form, letting the shapes be irregular.

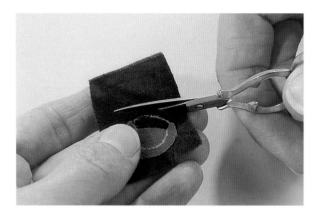

4. Continue adding shapes to each side of the first shape until you have stitched a body that is approximately 1½" long. Add a free-form, rounded head shape to the top, and a free-form, pointed tail shape to the bottom. Press the completed body unit.

Putting It All Together

1. Position the body unit on top of the stitched wings and appliqué it in place. For the tail, refer to "Steep Points" on page 19.

2. Press and trim the completed block, referring to "Finishing" on page 16.

Visit your local quilt shop and check out the various types of stencils available. You may find that a series of graduated oval shapes would make a beautiful body for this dragonfly. You can also find a wide variety of stencils with interesting shapes in art-supply stores. The possibilities are almost limitless, once you put your creativity in motion.

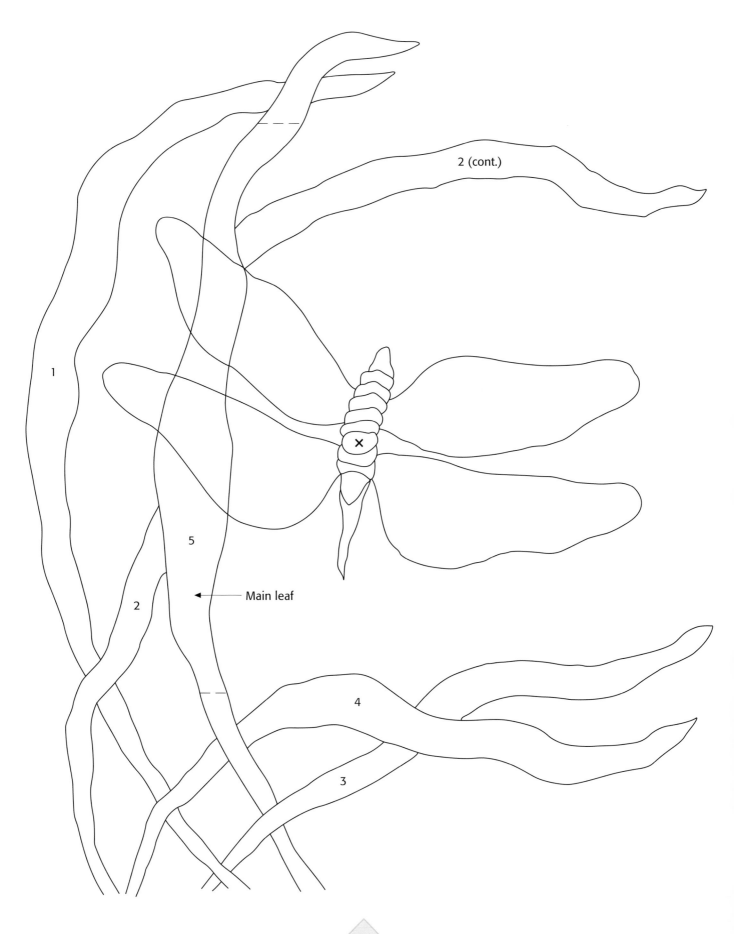

2 (cont.)

1

5

Main leaf

2

4

3

Damsel Moth

I used delicate metallic mesh and chiffon for the wings of this damsel moth. To make it look like nighttime, I chose dark colors for the free-form branches and a blended batik with subdued hues that echoed those in the body, head, and wings. Any see-through fabric you like will work for the upper and lower wing shapes.

Techniques

Free-form branches

Double reverse appliqué

Transparent appliqué

Working with specialty fabrics: metallic mesh, brocade, and tissue lamé

Beading

Fabrics and Supplies

- 11" square of fabric for background

- Two 11" squares of fabric for branches

- Fat quarter of blended batik or print fabric for leaves

- 4" x 8" piece of same background fabric as 11" square for large top-wing shape

- 4" x 8" piece of metallic mesh for large top-wing shape

- 4" x 6" piece of blended batik or print fabric for bottom wing shape

- 4" x 6" piece of metallic mesh for bottom wing shape

- 3" x 5" piece of blended batik or print fabric for small top-wing shape

- Scrap of brocade for body

- Scrap of tissue lamé for head

- Scrap of lightweight, fusible tricot interfacing (for tissue lamé)

- Cotton press cloth

- Seed beads for head

- Template plastic

- Sharpie permanent pen

Stitching the Branches and Leaves

1. Stitch the two-part free-form branches, referring to "Free-Form Stems and Branches" on page 18 and the photo on page 92. Stitch the completed branches onto the 11" background square. Press the background square.

2. Trace a leaf shape pattern from page 96 onto template plastic and cut it out. Mark around the template 16 times on the leaf fabric. Cut out each leaf with a ³⁄₁₆" seam allowance.

3. Appliqué the 16 leaves along the two branches, referring to "Starting to Stitch" on page 14. Press the background square.

Stitching the Top Wings

1. Trace both the small and large top-wing shapes from page 96 onto freezer paper and cut them out.

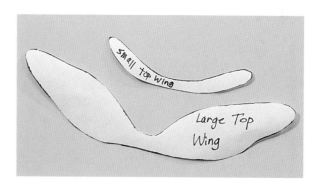

2. Press the template for the large top-wing shape onto the background square near the branches and leaves. Mark around the template and remove it. Cut a ³⁄₁₆" seam

allowance *inside* the marked lines of the large top wing.

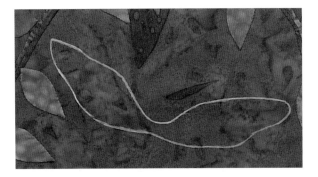

3. Press the small top-wing template onto the 4" x 8" piece of background fabric. Mark around the template and remove it. Cut a ³⁄₁₆" seam allowance *inside* the shape. Referring to the photo on page 92, place the 3" x 5" piece of batik or other fabric underneath the cut shape and reverse appliqué the small top-wing shape to the lower layer of fabric.

4. Place the 4" x 8" piece of metallic mesh on top of the background piece with the small top-wing shape appliquéd on it.

5. Place the layered fabrics from step 4 underneath the cut-out large top-wing shape on the background square, centering the small top-wing shape inside the large one. Pin the layers of fabric together.

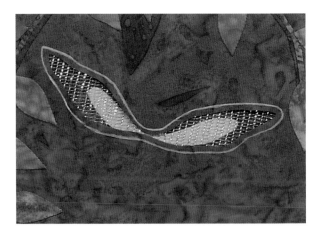

6. Referring to "Starting to Stitch" on page 14, reverse appliqué the large top-wing shape to the lower layers of fabric. On the wrong side of your work, trim the lower layers of fabric to ³⁄₁₆" from your stitched lines.

Stitching the Bottom Wings

1. Trace the bottom wing shape from page 96 onto freezer paper and cut it out.

2. Press the bottom wing template onto the background square, just beneath the stitched top wing. Mark around the template and remove it. Cut a ³⁄₁₆" seam allowance *inside* the wing shape.

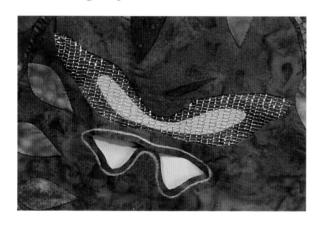

3. Place the 4" x 6" piece of metallic mesh on top of the 4" x 6" piece of batik or cotton print fabric.

4. Place the background square on top of the fabrics from step 3 and pin the layers together. Reverse appliqué the bottom wings to the lower layers of fabric, referring to "Starting to Stitch" on page 14 and the photo on page 92.

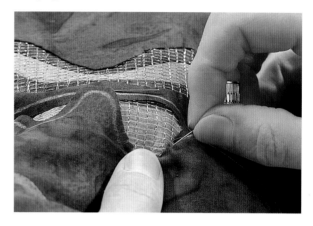

Putting It All Together

1. With a cotton press cloth on top, press a scrap of lightweight, fusible tricot interfacing to the wrong side of the scrap of tissue lamé.

2. Trace the body and head shapes from page 96 onto freezer paper and cut them out. With a cotton press cloth, press the body template onto the brocade fabric and the head template onto the fused tissue lamé. Mark around each template and remove them. Cut the body and head shapes out with a ³⁄₁₆" seam allowance.

3. Stitch the body and head shapes over the wings on the background square. Press and trim the completed background square with the cotton press cloth on top, referring to "Finishing" on page 16.

4. Thread a needle with thread that matches the seed beads you have chosen. Stitch the beads around the head.

TOP OF BLOCK

Luna Moth

One summer evening, I noticed a luna moth light on a tree trunk. Its icy green wings and brownish "eyes" were iridescent and gorgeous in the early moonlight. That magnificent creature eventually found its way into appliqué. Choose a dark background to simulate a deep forest at night, and pale, clear greens to make the wings luminous.

Techniques

Color blending

Unit appliqué

Free-form branches

Transparent appliqué

Reverse appliqué

Working with specialty fabrics:
    metallic sheers

Steep points

Fabrics and Supplies

- 11" square of fabric for background
- Four 11" squares of fabric for branches
- 6" x 8" piece of fabric for top wing
- 6" x 8" piece of fabric for narrow band of color on top wing
- 6" square of fabric for stems
- Six 4" x 6" bias pieces of fabric for bottom wing, body, tail, and antennae centers
- Two 2" x 4" pieces of same background fabric as 11" square for areas underneath antennae
- Two 2" x 4" pieces of metallic sheer fabric for areas underneath antennae
- Two 3" squares of same background fabric as 11" square for "eyes"
- Two 3" squares of metallic sheer fabric for "eyes"
- Two 2" squares of contrast fabric for "eyes"
- ¾" x 4" piece of fabric for antennae centers
- 2 scraps of print fabric with wavy circle motifs for "eyes"
- Assorted scraps of fabric for leaves
- Template plastic
- Sharpie permanent pen
- Cotton press cloth

Stitching the Branches and Leaves

1. To create the narrow, free-form stems, use your thumbnail and finger to fold two creases along the diagonal of the stem fabric square.

2. Cut a ⅛" seam allowance on each side of the creases. Cut the fabric into six 1"-long stems.

3. Referring to "Free-Form Stems and Branches" on page 18, stitch the two four-part, free-form branches, inserting the six stems into the seam allowances as you build up the branch.

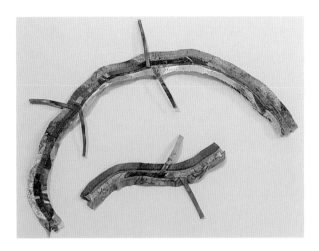

4. Referring to the photo on page 97, stitch the completed branches and stems onto the background square, leaving enough room for the luna moth between the stems.

5. Trace a leaf shape pattern from page 104 onto template plastic and cut it out. Mark around the template eight times on the leaf fabrics. Cut out each leaf with a ³⁄₁₆" seam allowance.

6. Appliqué the eight leaves along the two branches, referring to "Starting to Stitch" on page 14 and the photo on page 97. Press the background square.

Stitching the Top Wing

1. Trace the top wing pattern from page 103 onto freezer paper and cut it out. Cut carefully along the outer lines of the "eyes." Lay

the remaining portions of the eye templates aside temporarily.

2. Press the top wing template onto the right side of the fabric for the top wing and mark around it, including the eye openings. Remove the freezer-paper template and cut a ³⁄₁₆" seam allowance around the top wing. Leave the eyes intact temporarily.

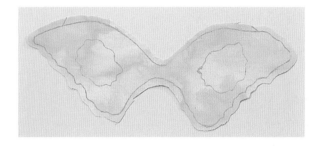

3. Stitch the top edge of the top wing to a piece of fabric for the narrow band of contrast color. Begin and end this stitching line approximately 1" in from the edges of the wings. Trim the contrast fabric to ¼" from the stitched line and approximately ⅛" beyond the first and last stitches.

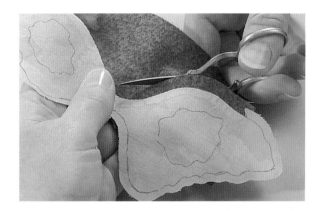

4. Cut a ³⁄₁₆" seam allowance *inside* one of the marked eye openings. Place a 3" square of metallic sheer fabric on top of a 3" square of background fabric and place these two layers of fabric underneath the cut eye opening. Reverse appliqué the eye opening to the lower layers of fabric. Repeat for the other marked eye opening.

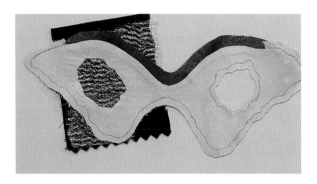

5. Cut the middle eye shape from the remaining eye shape of each eye template set aside in step 1. Press the templates on the corresponding contrast and wavy circle motif fabrics, and mark around them. Referring to the photo on page 97, stitch the middle and inner shapes inside each eye.

Stitching the Bottom Wing

1. Trace the bottom wing and tail shapes from page 103 onto freezer paper, including the hatch marks and numbers, and cut them out.

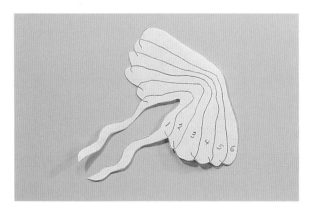

2. Cut shape 1 from the template and press it onto the tail fabric. Mark around the template. Make hatch marks that align with the ones on the template, and remove the template. Cut a ³⁄₁₆" seam allowance around shape 1, leaving the area between the two narrow shapes intact.

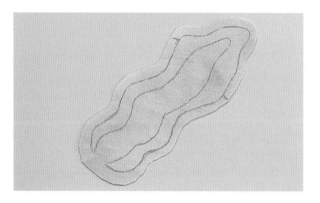

3. Clip the seam allowance to the marked line at each hatch mark. Turn under the seam allowance between the hatch marks and stitch this portion of shape 1 to the fabric for bottom-wing shape 2. Cut shape 2 from the pattern and press it next to the stitched seam. Mark around shape 2. Make hatch marks that align with the ones on the template, and remove the template. Cut a ³⁄₁₆" seam allowance around shape 2.

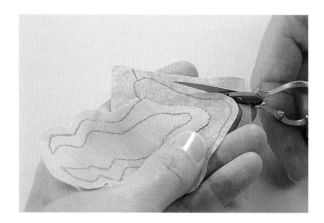

4. Repeat steps 2 and 3 above to add the remaining shapes of the bottom wing. Press the completed bottom wing.

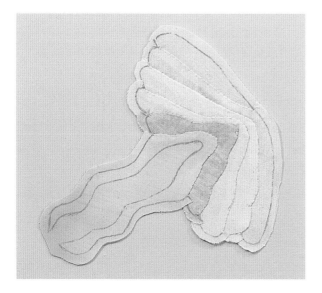

Putting It All Together

1. Trace the body shape from page 103 onto freezer paper and cut it out. Press the template onto the right side of the fabric for the body and mark around it. Remove the freezer-paper template and cut the body out with a ³⁄₁₆" seam allowance around it.

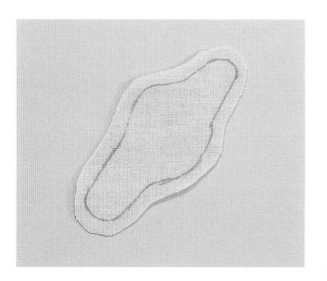

2. Arrange the top wing units, the bottom wing units, and the body between the leaves of the branches on the background square, as desired. Remove the top wing unit and body. Stitch the bottom wing unit to the background square, referring to "Starting to Stitch" on page 14 and "Steep Points" on page 19.

3. Stitch the top wing unit to the background square, overlapping the bottom wing. Stitch the body on top of the wings. Press the background square.

4. Layer the two 2" x 4" pieces of metallic sheer fabric on top of the two 2" x 4" pieces of background fabric. Lay one pair of layered fabrics aside temporarily.

5. Place the ³⁄₄" x 4" piece of antennae-center fabric along the long edge of the layered metallic sheer and background fabrics from step 4. Using a ruler and a quilter's pencil (or a Hera marker), mark a seam line on the antennae-center fabric. Hand piece the three layers of fabric together with a short running stitch.

6. Fold the antennae-center strip under so that only ¹⁄₁₆" is visible.

7. Open the pieces so that the antennae-center strip is right side out.

8. Pin the fabric to the remaining layered metallic sheer and background strips. Appliqué the edge of the antennae center to the layered strips.

9. Trace the two antennae shapes from page 103 onto freezer paper and cut them out. Press the templates on the background square so that the points touch the luna moth's head. Mark around the templates and remove the freezer paper. Cut a ¹⁄₈" seam allowance inside one antenna shape (see photo on page 97).

10. Position and pin the layered antennae-center fabrics from step 8 underneath the cut antenna opening. Reverse appliqué the edges of the antenna opening to the lower layers of fabric, referring to the photo on page 97. Repeat for the second antenna. Trim the lower layers of fabric to ³⁄₁₆" from your stitched lines.

11. Press and trim the completed block, referring to "Finishing" on page 16.

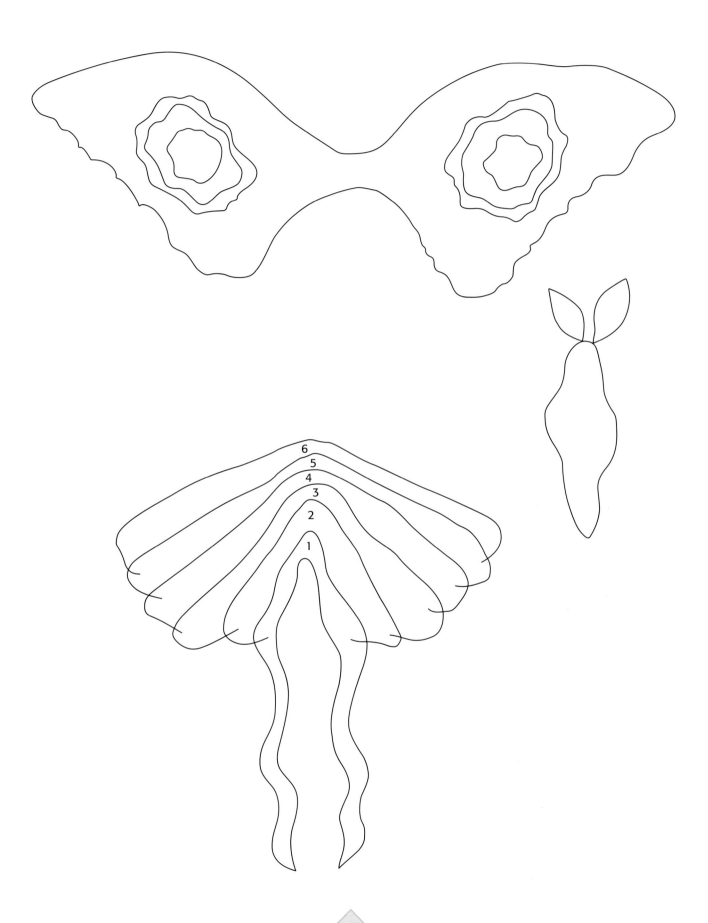

TOP OF BLOCK

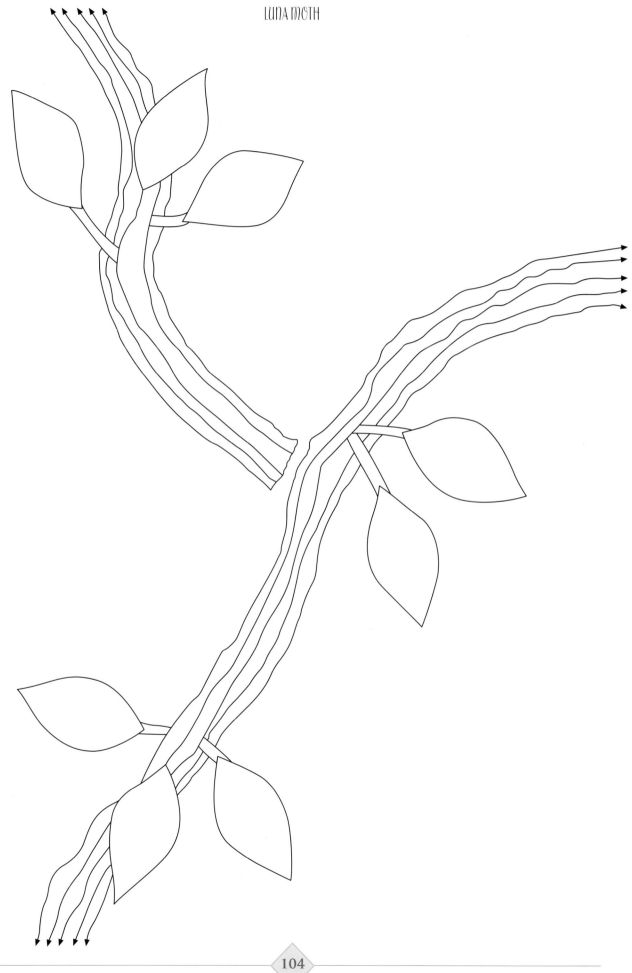

Cicada Moth

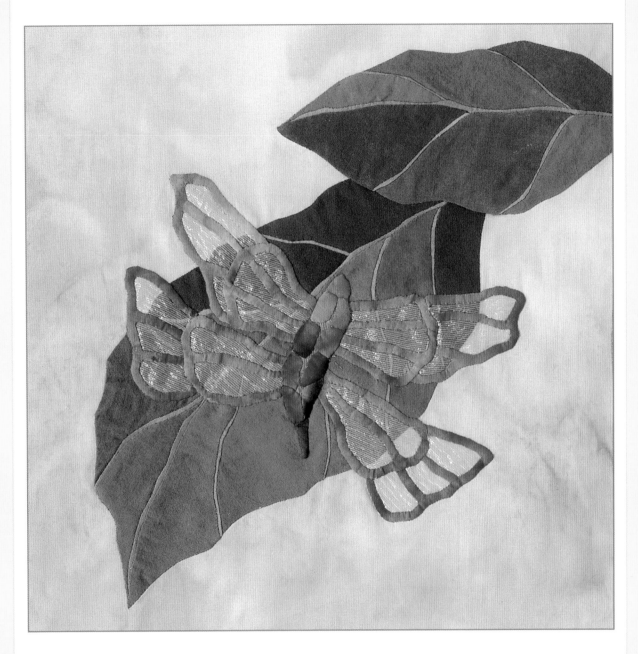

Here I've combined a blended batik with a textured metallic sheer fabric to create the transparent wings of a cicada moth. The trick is to reverse appliqué the batik to the sheer fabric so that the seam allowances will not be visible in your finished work.

Techniques

Color blending

Unit appliqué

Sandwiching narrow bands of color between shapes

Transparent appliqué

Working with specialty fabrics: metallic sheers

Steep points

Fabrics and Supplies

- 11" square of fabric for background
- 11" square of metallic sheer fabric for wings and body
- 11" square of blended batik fabric for wings and body
- Fat quarter of fabric (or assorted scraps) for leaf veins
- Assorted 6" squares of fabric for leaves
- Glue stick
- Cotton press cloth

Stitching the Leaves

1. Trace the large leaf pattern from page 111 onto freezer paper, including the numbers, and cut it out.

2. Cut shape 1 from the large leaf pattern and press it onto the right side of the fabric for this shape. Mark around shape 1. Remove the freezer-paper template and cut shape 1 out with a ³⁄₁₆" seam allowance.

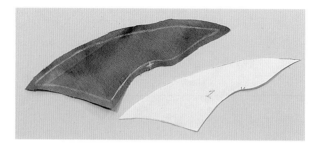

3. On shape 1, clip the seam allowance in the inner curved area. Turn the seam allowance under and stitch this edge of shape 1 to the leaf-vein fabric.

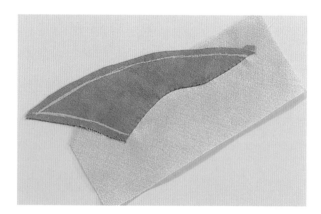

4. Trim the leaf-vein fabric to a scant ¼" from the stitched line. Also trim away the excess vein fabric underneath shape 1.

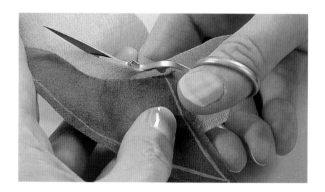

5. Turn under the leaf-vein fabric so that only about ¹⁄₁₆" is visible and stitch it to a piece of fabric for shape 2.

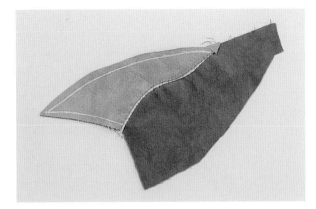

6. Cut shape 2 from the pattern and press it next to the stitched line on shape 1, overlapping the leaf vein, so that you do not widen shape 2 by the width of the vein. Mark around shape 2 as shown, and then remove the template. Cut out shape 2 with a ³⁄₁₆" seam allowance.

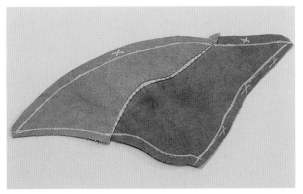

7. Repeat steps 2–6 to add shapes 3, 4, and 5 with veins. Press the completed lower half of the large leaf unit. Construct the top half of the leaf in the same manner. Stitch the top edge of the lower leaf unit to the leaf-vein fabric. Cut the leaf-vein fabric to ¼" from your stitched line. Turn under the leaf-vein fabric so that only about ¹⁄₁₆" is visible and appliqué it to the top half of the leaf.

8. Repeat steps 1–7 to stitch the small leaf unit.

Stitching the Wings

1. Trace the wing patterns from page 110 onto freezer paper and cut them out, including the openings.

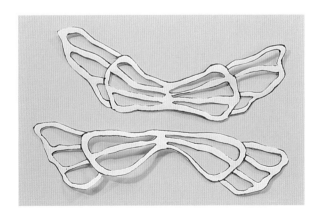

2. Cut the two outer portions from the bottom wing pattern.

3. Press the center portion of the template onto the right side of the blended batik fabric. Mark around the template, including the openings. Remove the freezer-paper template and cut the shape out with a ³⁄₁₆" seam allowance, including inside the openings.

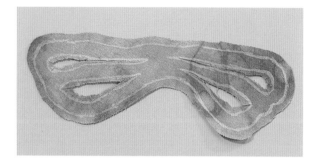

4. Clip the seam allowances at the inner curved areas inside each opening. At each opening, turn under and crease the seam allowance. Glue-baste the seam allowance in position on the wrong side of the shape.

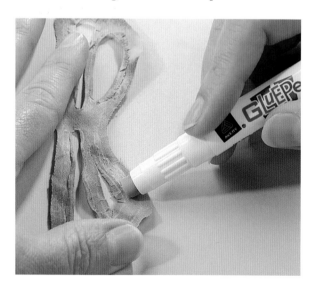

5. Run the glue stick lightly over the wrong side of the bottom center-wing shape and finger-press it onto a layer of metallic sheer fabric. Trim the metallic sheer fabric even with the edges of the bottom center-wing shape.

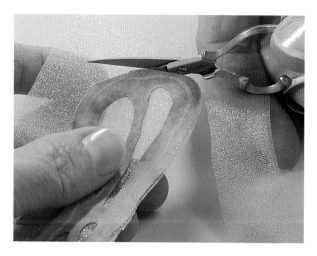

6. Repeat steps 3–4 for the two outer portions of the bottom wing.

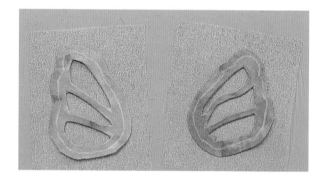

7. Place the bottom center-wing shape over the two outer portions of the bottom wing. Turn under the edges of the center-wing shape and take a few short stitches to tack them to the batik fabric of the outer portions.

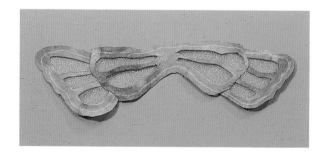

8. Repeat steps 3–6 for the top wing shape.

Stitching the Body

1. Trace the body pattern from page 110 onto freezer paper and cut it out.

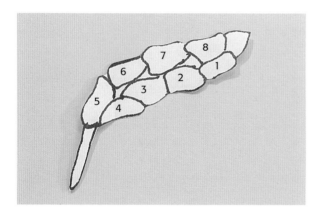

2. Layer a piece of metallic sheer fabric on top of a piece of blended batik fabric; both must be large enough to accommodate the entire body unit. Cut the head and tail pieces from the pattern and press them onto the right side of a different piece of batik fabric. Mark around the head and tail pieces, remove them, and cut them out with a ³⁄₁₆" seam allowance around them. Stitch the head and tail pieces to the first two layered metallic sheer and batik fabrics. Cut the shape 1 template from the freezer-paper pattern and press it onto the batik fabric. Mark around the template. Remove the freezer-paper template and cut shape 1 out with a ³⁄₁₆" seam allowance around it. Stitch the top, inner, and bottom edges of shape 1 to the layered metallic sheer and batik fabrics, leaving the outer edge free.

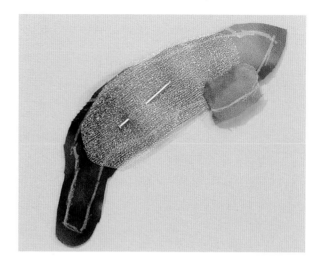

3. Stitch body shapes 2 through 8 in the same manner as shape 1, allowing bits of the metallic sheer fabric to peek out between the shapes. Trim the layered metallic sheer and batik fabrics even with the edges of the body pieces. Stitch the lower edges of shapes 4 and 5 to the tail.

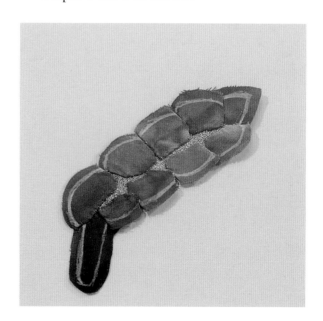

Putting It All Together

1. Arrange the leaf units on the background square. Referring to "Steep Points" on page 19, stitch the leaves in place. Press the background square.

2. Position and stitch the top and bottom wing units over the leaves, referring to the photo on page 105.

3. Position and stitch the body unit over the wings, referring to the photo on page 105.

4. Press and trim the completed block, referring to "Finishing" on page 16. Use a cotton press cloth to protect the metallic sheer fabric.

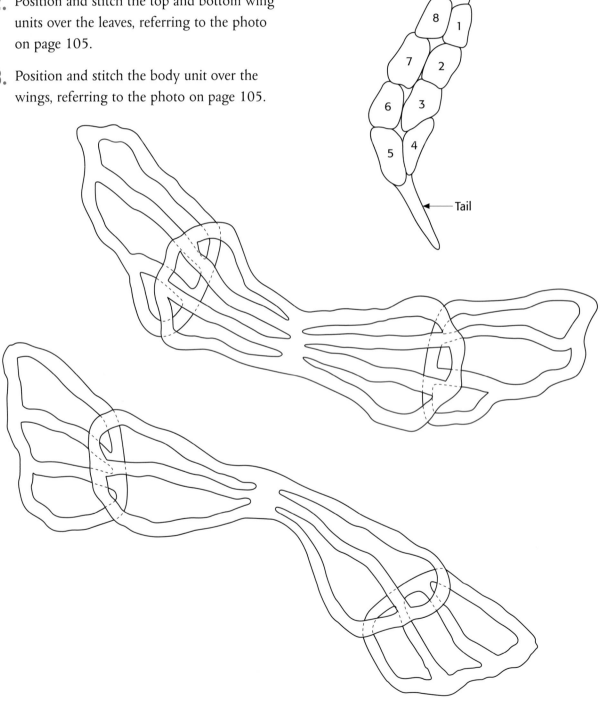

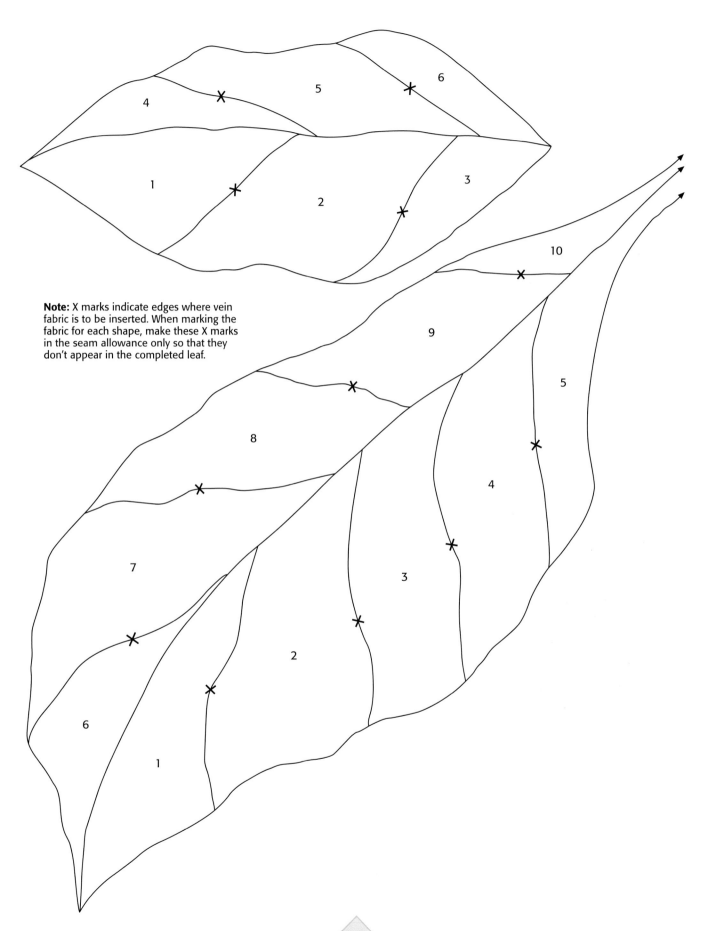

Note: X marks indicate edges where vein fabric is to be inserted. When marking the fabric for each shape, make these X marks in the seam allowance only so that they don't appear in the completed leaf.

Forrester Butterfly

A layer of black fabric is reverse appliquéd over the top of several color-blended greens in the wings of this butterfly. Whether you make your butterfly in the colors I used or choose others, use similar value fabrics for the color-blended layer and a highly contrasting fabric for the top layer of the wings.

Techniques

Unit appliqué

Reverse appliqué on top of color-blend appliqué

Hera bias stems

Edging shapes with narrow bands of color

Steep points

Inking

Fabrics and Supplies

- 11" square of fabric for background
- Three 9" squares of fabric for leaves
- 9" square of fabric for body and reverse appliqué (top) layer of wings
- 6" square of fabric for stem
- Ten 3" squares of fabric for flower
- Assorted scrap fabrics for color-blend portions of wings and contrast for body
- Black Pigma permanent-marking pen

Stitching the Flower

1. Place the square of stem fabric wrong side up on a cutting mat. Referring to "Bias Stems and Vines" on page 17, cut a ¼" x 7" stem.

2. Trace the flower unit pattern from page 118 onto freezer paper, including the hatch marks, and cut it out.

3. Cut petal shape 1 from the pattern and press it onto the right side of the first flower fabric. Mark around petal shape 1. Also make hatch marks that align with the ones on the template.

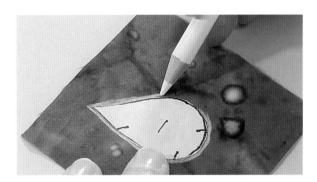

4. Remove the freezer-paper template and cut a ³⁄₁₆" seam allowance around petal shape 1. Clip the seam allowance to the marked line at each hatch mark. Stitch petal shape 1 to the fabric for petal shape 2, beginning and ending at the hatch marks at the rounded end of the shape.

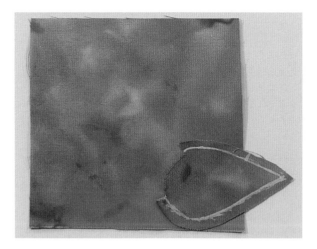

5. Cut petal shape 2 from the pattern and press it next to the stitched line on petal shape 1. Mark around petal shape 2, including the hatch marks.

6. Remove the freezer-paper template and cut petal shape 2 out with a ³⁄₁₆" seam allowance around it.

7. Clip the seam allowance at the hatch mark on petal shape 2. Stitch petal shapes 1 and 2 to the fabric for petal shape 3, beginning and ending at the hatch marks on each shape. Repeat steps 5 and 6 to add petal shape 3 to the flower unit.

8. Referring to steps 3–7, continue adding petal shapes 4 through 10. Press the completed flower unit.

Stitching the Leaves

1. Trace and number the two-part leaf pattern from page 118 onto freezer paper and cut it out. Cut the leaf pattern apart on the marked line.

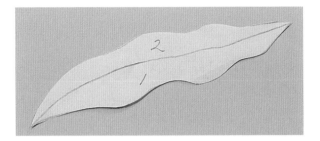

2. Press the template for leaf shape 1 onto a leaf fabric. Mark around the template. Remove the freezer-paper template and cut a 3/16" seam allowance around leaf shape 1. Stitch the long edge of leaf shape 1 to the fabric for leaf shape 2.

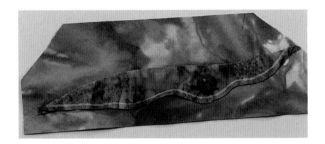

3. Press the template for leaf shape 2 next to the stitched line on leaf shape 1. Mark around leaf shape 2, remove the freezer-paper template, and cut the shape out with a 3/16" seam allowance around it. Trim the excess fabric underneath to 3/16" from your stitched line. Press the completed leaf unit.

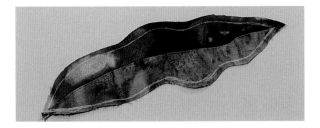

4. Trace the single leaf pattern from page 118 onto freezer paper and cut it out. Press the template onto the right side of a leaf fabric and mark around it. Remove the freezer-paper template and cut the single leaf out with a 3/16" seam allowance around it.

Stitching the Wings

1. Trace the two numbered patterns for the color-blended portions of the bottom left and right wings from page 119 onto freezer paper and cut them out.

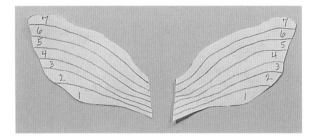

2. Cut wing shape 1 from the left-wing pattern and press it onto the right side of the fabric for this shape. Mark around wing shape 1, remove the freezer-paper template, and cut the shape out with a 3/16" seam allowance around it. Stitch the top edge of wing shape 1 to the fabric for wing shape 2.

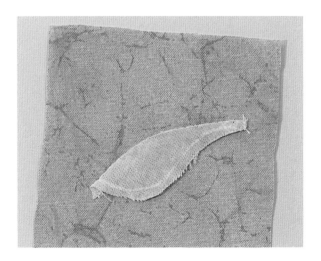

3. Cut wing shape 2 from the pattern and press it next to the stitched line on wing shape 1. Mark around wing shape 2, remove the template, and cut out the shape with a ³⁄₁₆" seam allowance around it.

4. Repeat steps 2 and 3 to add wing shapes 3 through 6. Press the completed color-blend unit for the bottom left wing.

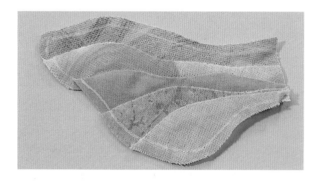

5. Repeat steps 2–4 to stitch the color-blend portion of the bottom right wing.

6. Trace the reverse appliqué shape for the bottom left wing from page 119 onto freezer paper and cut it out, including the area inside the opening.

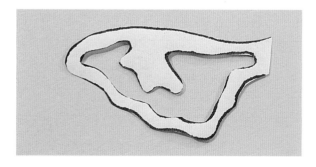

7. Press the reverse appliqué template onto the 9" square of contrast fabric. Mark around the template, including the edges of the opening. Remove the freezer-paper template.

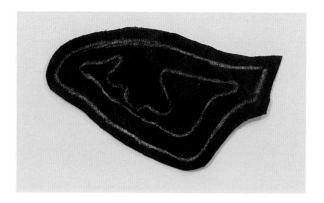

8. Cut midway through the narrowest seam allowances, and then continue cutting inside the wing shape, leaving ⅛" seam allowances.

9. Place the reverse appliqué shape on top of the color-blend unit for the bottom left wing and stitch the edges of the opening to the lower layer. On the wrong side of the wing shape, trim the lower color-blend layer to ³⁄₁₆" from your stitched line. Press the completed bottom left-wing unit.

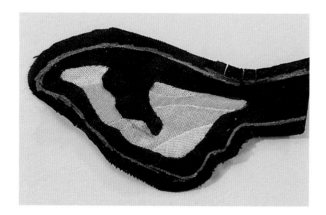

10. Complete the bottom right-wing unit, referring to steps 6–9 on page 116. Stitch the top left-wing unit and top right-wing unit in the same manner. Press the completed wing units.

Stitching the Body

1. Trace the body pattern from page 119 onto freezer paper, including the hatch marks, and cut it out. Cut the largest body shape from the pattern and press it onto the right side of the body fabric. Mark around the shape, including the hatch marks, and remove the freezer-paper template. Cut the shape out with a 3/16" seam allowance around it. Clip the hatch marks and stitch the curved sides of the shape to the body contrast fabric for the narrow band of color.

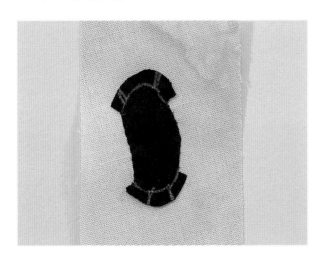

2. Trim the contrast fabric to a scant 1/4" from your stitched lines.

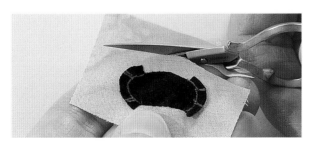

3. Stitch the remaining body shapes to the large shape, referring to steps 1 and 2 and the photo on page 112. Press the completed body unit.

Putting It All Together

1. Arrange the stem, leaves, flower unit, wing units, and body unit on the background square, referring to the photo on page 112.

2. Referring to "Starting to Stitch" on page 14, stitch the shapes onto the background square in the following order: the stem, the single leaf and the two-part leaf (refer to "Steep Points" on page 19), the flower unit, the wing units, and the body unit.

3. Using the Pigma pen, draw the antennae above the head.

4. Press and trim the completed block, referring to "Finishing" on page 16.

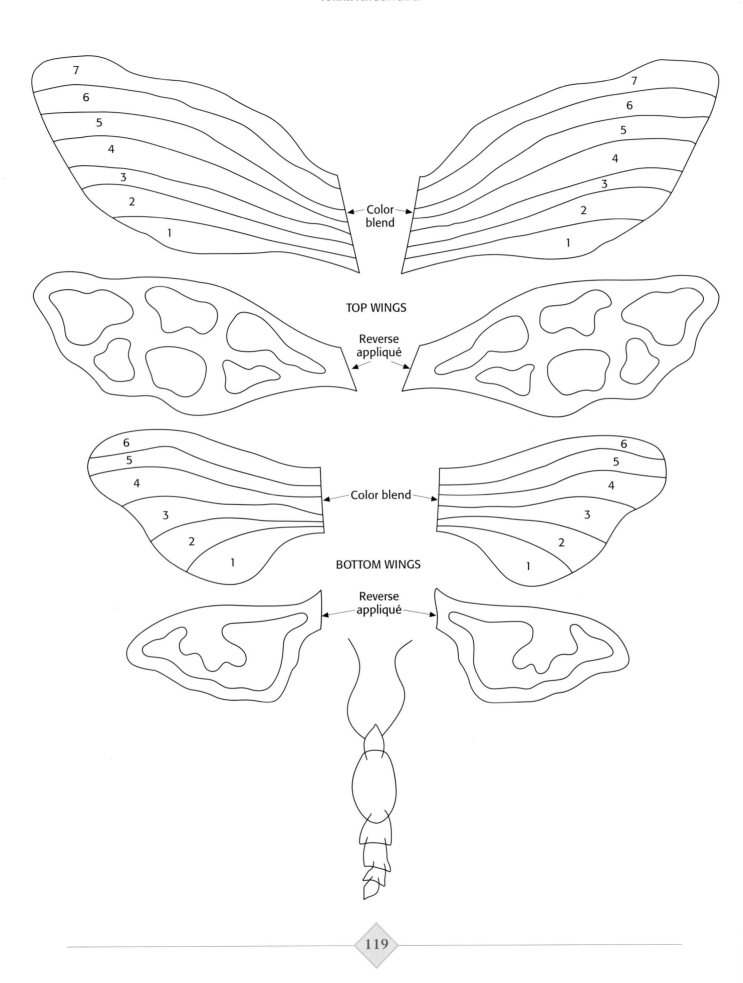

TOP WINGS

Color blend

Reverse appliqué

BOTTOM WINGS

Color blend

Reverse appliqué

Monarch Butterfly

The monarch butterfly is one of the most beautiful in North America, drawing attention to its yellowish orange wings against the lush greens of nature. Although you might think, at first glance, that the details on this butterfly are embroidered, they involve just simple appliqué.

Techniques

Color blending

Unit appliqué

Two-part background square

Sandwiching narrow bands of color between appliqué shapes

Working with specialty fabrics: textured polyester knit

Inking

Beading

Fabrics and Supplies

- One 11" square of fabric for center portion of block
- One 11" square of fabric for background
- Fat quarter of dark fabric for tail, head, narrow bands of contrast color, and outer edges of butterfly
- Assorted 6" squares of fabric for wings
- 3" square of textured polyester knit fabric (or other fabric) for body
- Seed beads
- White gel roller pen
- Removable or air-soluble marking pen
- Clear nail polish
- Cotton press cloth

Stitching the Background Square

1. Trace the curved lines of the background square pattern on page 126 onto an 11" square of freezer paper, making sure that the lines go all the way to the edges of the paper. Include the cross mark that indicates the block center on the freezer paper. To avoid any confusion, include the words *top, center, left,* and *right.*

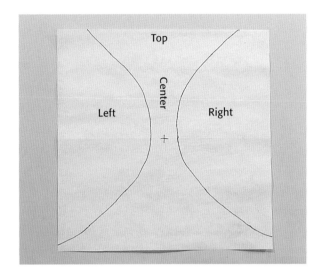

2. Cut the square of freezer paper apart on the curved lines. Press the center portion on the right side of the fabric for this shape. Mark the shape on the fabric. Remove the freezer paper and cut a ¾6" seam allowance around the shape. Clip the seam allowances along the curved lines.

3. Layer the center portion on top of the 11" square of background fabric. Stitch the curved edges of the center portion to the lower layer. Press the completed background square.

Stitching the Top Wing

1. Trace the top wing shape from page 125 onto freezer paper, including the numbers and *excluding* the outermost line.

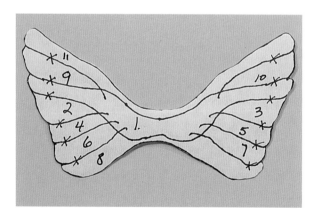

2. Cut wing shape 1 from the pattern and press it onto the right side of the fabric for this shape. Mark around wing shape 1. Also make hatch marks that align with the ones on the template. The X marks indicate where narrow bands of black fabric will be inserted. Transfer the Xs to the seam allowance when marking the fabric. Remove the template, and then cut the shape out with a ³⁄₁₆" seam allowance around it. Also, using a removable or air-soluble marking pen, mark the hatch marks on wing shape 1.

3. Stitch the long edges of wing shape 1 to the dark fat quarter for contrast.

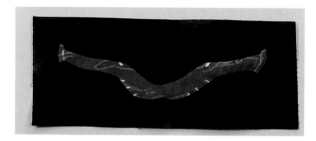

4. Trim the contrast fabric to ¼" from your stitched lines on both long sides of shape 1. Turn under the contrast fabric so that only about ¹⁄₁₆" is visible on the bottom edge, and finger-crease the fold. Stitch the edge of the contrast fabric to the fabric for shape 2, referring to the pattern on page 125. Stop this stitching line exactly at the first hatch mark.

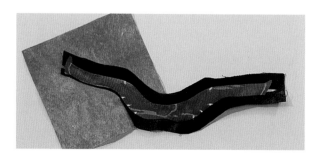

5. Cut wing shape 2 from the freezer-paper pattern and press it next to the stitched line on wing shape 1 so that it overlaps the narrow band of contrast fabric. Mark around wing shape 2, remove the freezer-paper template, and cut the shape out with a ³⁄₁₆" seam allowance around it. On the wrong side of your work, trim excess fabric from shape 2 to ³⁄₁₆" from the stitching line.

6. Stitch the long edge of wing shape 2 to the contrast fabric. Trim the contrast fabric to a scant ¼" from the stitched line as shown.

7. Turn under the contrast fabric along the other lower edge of wing shape 1 so that only about ¹⁄₁₆" is visible, and finger-crease the fold. Stitch this edge of the contrast fabric to the fabric for wing shape 3.

8. Repeat step 5 to mark and cut a ³⁄₁₆" seam allowance around wing shape 3. Repeat step 6 to stitch wing shape 3 to the contrast fabric. Turn under and finger-crease the contrast fabric so that only ¹⁄₁₆" is visible. Referring to steps 2–7 and the photo on page 120, continue adding wing shapes 4 through 11, with narrow bands of contrast color between each shape. Press the completed top wing unit.

Stitching the Reverse-Appliqué Spots and the Edges of the Top Wing

1. Trace the reverse appliqué areas of the top wings from page 125 onto freezer paper.

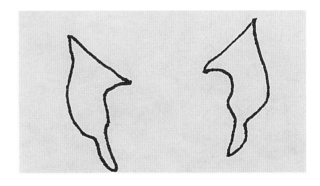

2. Press the reverse appliqué templates on top of the top wing unit, referring to the photo on page 120. Mark around the edges of the templates and remove them.

3. Carefully cut a ³⁄₁₆" seam allowance *inside* the marked lines.

4. Referring to the photo on page 120, stitch the reverse appliqué areas to a lower layer of contrast fabric. Using the white gel roller pen, mark several small ovals along the outer edges of each reverse appliqué spot. Add a small drop of clear nail polish to each oval to seal the ink and keep it from smearing. Allow the nail polish to dry. Stitch the top wing unit to a piece of dark contrast fabric. Trace the outer lines of the top wing from page 125 onto an 8" square of freezer paper and cut the outer wing shape from the square to create a window template. Press the window template over the stitched top wing and mark the curved outer edges of the top wing. Remove the freezer-paper template and cut a ³⁄₁₆" seam allowance around the top wing. Add small oval spots along the outer edges of the top wing. Use clear nail polish to seal these spots and let them dry.

Stitching the Bottom Wing

Referring to "Stitching the Top Wing" on pages 122–123, stitch the bottom wing unit in the same manner.

Stitching the Body

1. Trace the body pattern from page 125 onto freezer paper and cut it out. Cut the largest body shape from the pattern. Press it onto the right side of the textured polyester knit fabric using a cotton press cloth. Mark around the shape, remove the template, and then cut out the shape with a ⅛" seam allowance.

2. Stitch the top edge of the large body shape to the fabric for the head. Press the head template next to the stitched line and mark around it. Remove the freezer paper and cut a ³⁄₁₆" seam allowance around the head.

3. Repeat step 2 to add the four tail pieces to the large body shape. With a cotton press cloth on top, press the completed body unit.

Putting It All Together

1. Referring to the photo on page 120, arrange and stitch the bottom and top wing units on the background square, followed by the body unit.

2. Using the removable or air-soluble marking pen, add the lines of the antennae onto the background square. You do not need to trace the lines; you can draw them freehand. Using thread that matches the beads, stitch seed beads along each of the antennae lines.

3. Press and trim the completed block, referring to "Finishing" on page 16. Take care to avoid the seed beads when pressing.

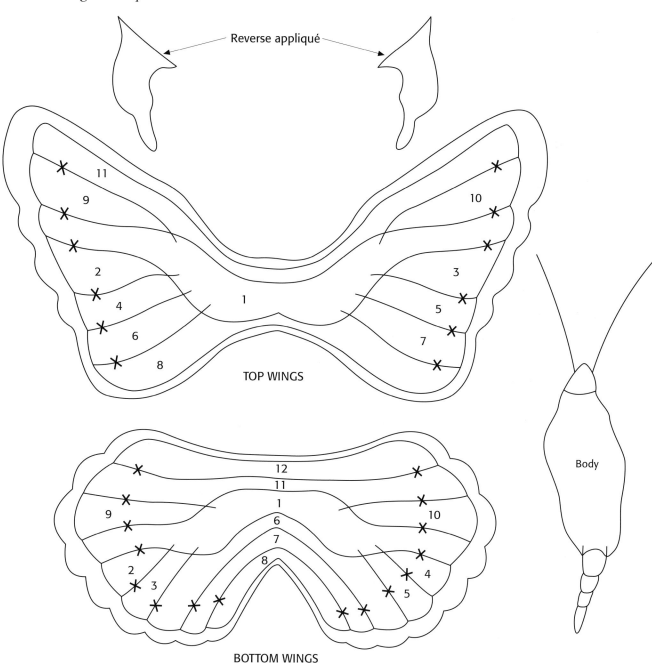

Reverse appliqué

TOP WINGS

BOTTOM WINGS

Body

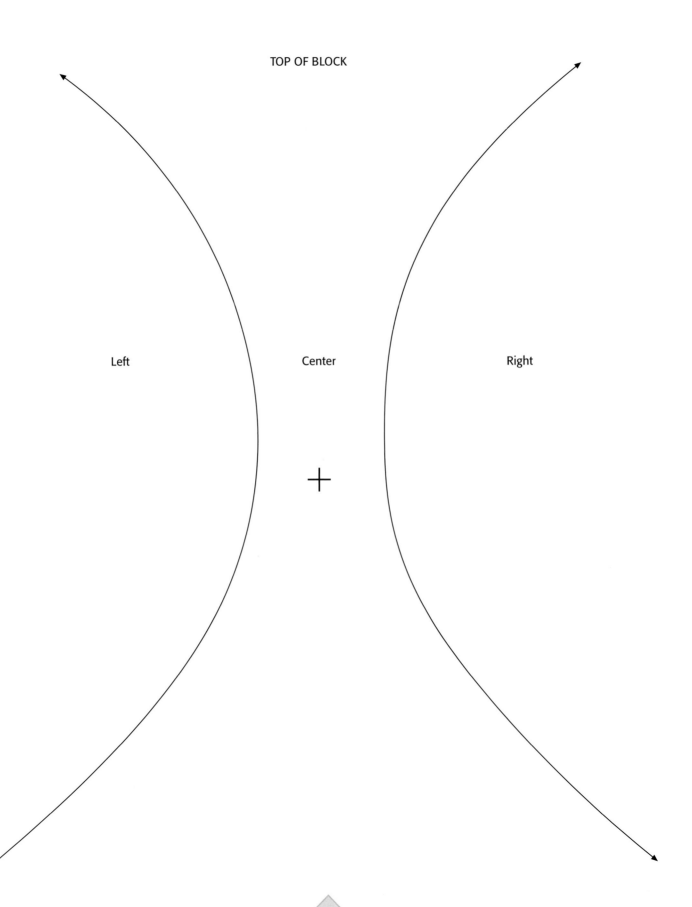

TOP OF BLOCK

Left   Center   Right

Resources

Gail Kessler
Ladyfingers Sewing Studio
6375 Oley Turnpike Rd., Oley, PA 19547
Phone: 610-689-0068
Fax: 610-689-0067
General sewing supplies, quilt fabrics, block-of-the month kits, 3½" serrated embroidery scissors, CAT paper, 100-denier YLI silk thread (all colors), John James needles

Jeana Kimball's Foxglove Cottage
P.O. Box 698
Santa Clara, UT 84765
Check your local quilt shop or contact Foxglove Cottage directly for size 11 straw needles.

Mickey Lawler's Skydyes
P.O. Box 370116
West Hartford, CT 06137-0116
Email: Skydyes@aol.com
Web site: www.skydyes.com
Phone: 860-232-1429
Fax: 860-236-9117

Jane Townswick
For information on workshop and lecture offerings, contact Jane Townswick at jtown@enter.net.

About the Author

Jane Townswick is an accomplished author, editor, teacher, and former quilt shop owner. She has been an instructor at the esteemed Elly Sienkiewicz Appliqué Academy since 2000 and her work has been featured in *Quilter's Newsletter Magazine* and *American Quilter* magazine. She is the author of three books published by Martingale & Company, including *Color-Blend Appliqué* (2003). Jane lives in Allentown, Pennsylvania, and lectures and teaches workshops throughout the country. To contact her, see "Resources" on page 127.